Full Speed Ahead

Published By: Doctors Publishing Group, LLC

(Members of Doctors Publishing Group, LLC:

Dr. Sybil M. Deveaux, Dr. T. Andrew Elliott,

Dr. Leilani Longa, Dr. Melanie Magruder, Dr. Cheryl Szyarto,

Dr. Ed S. Turner III)

Authors: Dr. Sybil M. Deveaux, Dr. T. Andrew Elliott,

Dr. Leilani Longa, Dr. Melanie Magruder, Dr. Cheryl Szyarto,

Dr. Ed S. Turner III

Editor: Crawford Editing and Consulting

Collaborative Editor: Dr. Melanie Magruder

Cover Design: Designonomy, Inc.

ISBN-13: 978-1456300678

ISBN-10: 1456300679

Reviews for *Full Speed Ahead*

Welcome to the rapidly expanding world of online education! What was once unconventional is now a readily accepted means for educational connections and experience. This book gives fantastic insight from both research and practical experience that illuminates the online doctoral path in a manner that is both accessible and realistic. It is a "how to," from the beginning steps to the realization of a dream fueled by the technology available to support those who are excited about and interested in reaching new heights in personal and professional growth through the online experience. From the process of picking an institution, through all the hurdles along the way, the authors have presented sound advice based on both professional findings and personal connections. The style and approach is one that makes the topic both informative and enjoyable as readers add to their understanding of and connection to an important topic for anyone considering this venture.

Dr. Lori Curci-Reed
Campus College Chair, College of Education
University of Phoenix, Southern California Campus

Full Speed Ahead is a GPS for all learners at any stage along their doctoral journey. Travelers would not begin their road trip without a map or GPS to guide them to a specific destination. Similarly, graduate learners should not embark on a doctoral journey without considering the time involved and investigating the intellectual, emotional, and financial investment involved in achieving their goal. The authors of *Full Speed Ahead* have completed the doctoral road trip—and what a road they have traveled.

The authors provide the reader with the knowledge and skills they need to pack for their own doctoral road trip. The chapters present a background to the milestones the doctoral learner will encounter and show how each author navigated that challenge/landmark. The personal reflections shared by the authors provide the reader with a window into the authors' experiences. For example, "One Day in the Life of a Doctoral Student" clearly illustrates the challenge of balancing personal, professional, and academic responsibilities; another chapter illustrates the emotional benefit of the "priceless friendships" forged at residency. The collective experiences of the authors plot the course for future travelers in reaching their doctoral destination.

Dr. Glenda Black
Assistant Professor
Member, Northern Canadian Centre for Research in
    Education & the Arts (NORCCREA)
Schulich School of Education,
Nipissing University

Every doctoral student embarks upon an arduous journey. *Full Speed Ahead: Surviving to Thriving as an Online Doctoral Student* equips students with the detailed travel itinerary needed to guide them throughout this exciting voyage. From deciding "Is Online Learning for Me?" en route to "What's Next? Getting Published!" students are guided step-by-step, as well as cautioned about possible delays to their travel plans.

The personal experiences sections, located at the ends of many chapters, provide readers with a glimpse into each author's individual journey and provide encouragement to readers as they encounter setbacks along the way. In the words of one author, "I learned to accept that every step forward, however great or small, was a step in the right direction and was one step closer to program completion. No challenge would impede me from fulfilling my goal of successfully completing the doctoral program in which I was enrolled." *Full Speed Ahead:* is a must read for those who are seeking to fulfill their goal of successfully completing their online doctoral program!

Dr. A. Elena Bogardus
Associate Professor
Camden County College, New Jersey

Dedications

To the memory of Jim Olden Turner, my loving brother and confidant. The Lord took him from us far too soon. May he rest in peace.

Ed

To the next generation of our young scholars seeking to obtain their doctoral degree.

Leilani

To the eternal memory of my daughter, Racquel Kim Delancy, and my brother-in-law, Dennis George Waite.

Sybil (Ma)

To all the future students who think they may pursue a doctorate. May this book lead and guide you through a new and amazing learning process.

Andy

To the loving memory of my grandfather, Rocco De Francesco.

Cheryl

To grace and humility, for being priceless

Melanie

and...

To the loving memory of Jonathan L. Tex, who left us too soon, the son of one of our most prestigious colleagues, Nick Tex.

Introduction

F - Finally.....
U - Useful
L - Lighthearted
L - Language to...

S - Simplify and
P - Provide
E - Engaging and
E - Entertaining
D - Dialogue for....

A - Ardently
H - Helping and
E - Encouraging
A - Anyone in pursuit of a
D - Doctoral degree

Scholars of the 21st century need to be cognizant of the enormous technological strides educators have taken. Which system is better, the traditional classroom study or online learning? Do employers prefer one system over the other? How does online learning affect the value of a doctoral degree? Do I have time, and is online learning for me? What are the pros and cons of online learning? Will I be assigned a mentor or will I have to select one? Who determines the quality of my work? Will I have to defend my dissertation? These are typical questions asked of the online student.

Full Speed Ahead is a groundbreaking collaboration among six doctors who earned their degrees online. The doctors prove that earning a terminal degree is a matter of discipline and teamwork. Through storytelling, *Full Speed Ahead* educates the potential doctoral student about the entire process, beginning with a comparison of online versus traditional processes and ending with advice about how to get published.

The Greek philosopher Aristotle (384 BC - 322 BC) postulated that the best way to provide for old age is to get an education. Like many students who vacillate because of cost, time constraints, or personal issues, the typical learner worries. Chances are you fall within this category; however, *Full Speed Ahead* reveals the secrets to obtaining an online doctoral degree and achieving success.

Reading *Full Speed Ahead* will help you understand phrases and terminologies you would otherwise stumble over or question. Each chapter will make you want to turn the pages more quickly in order to find answers to the original questions posed in this introduction. Who knows? Sometime in the next four years you may be writing *Full Speed Ahead, Part II.*

Table of Contents

Chapter 1: Online and Traditional Doctoral Education

Ed S. Turner III

The history of education goes back to the earliest time when mankind strove to pass on social and cultural values, traditions, religion, morality, and all kinds of skills to the next generation. The earliest evidence of this is in the form of drawings on the rocks of ancient ruins. When writing was invented, it became possible for man to pass on knowledge, beliefs, and customs by accurately recording this information. Although it is not written in the Bible, it is clear that Jesus received an excellent education through the "school of the book," which was the synagogue in Nazareth where he spent his childhood, a precursor to formal education as we know it. His scholarship evolved into what is the basic learning tool in many homes throughout the world, the Holy Bible. Even today many children will receive their earliest education in the home based upon their parents' religious beliefs and deep-seated tradition with learning from the Koran (The Qur'an-Islam), Holy Bible,

Tanakh (Judaism), Tipitaka (Buddhism), and other basic religious and doctrinal books.

In one's effort to reach the highest echelons of education and receive that "terminal degree," which denotes the eminent degree one can obtain, many decide to obtain a doctorate. Although in certain circles a doctorate is considered a prerequisite to teach at the university level, there are also other considerations to obtaining a doctorate. There are several types of doctorates: research doctorate, highest doctorate, professional doctorate, and honorary doctorate. Increasingly, individuals are using doctoral education as a means for reaching the highest level of educational experience for professional positions in the workforce, such as MDs, DOs, and CEOs, as presidents of large corporations or other entities seek to obtain doctorates. Although one's expertise may already be recognized by many people, one may also find that obtaining a doctorate gives credibility to one's position. Unfortunately, this is one of the many wrong reasons for obtaining a doctorate.

So what does it take to obtain a doctorate, one might ask. Everyone who walks away from the doctoral experience has different thoughts on what it takes. For me answering that question was easy. It takes intelligence, time, creativity, intense curiosity, adaptability, self-motivation, competitiveness, and maturity. If you are ready and have what it takes, then let us start an exploration into the doctoral world.

History of the Traditional Doctoral Education Model

Before one can discuss the history of the traditional doctoral education model, it is necessary to understand what we are talking about. A doctorate is a professional or academic degree that qualifies holders to teach or conduct their profession in a specific field. The quest for a doctorate usually follows a bachelor's and master's degree. In most countries, a doctorate is the highest degree given in a field and is frequently referred to as a terminal degree. Traditional doctoral candidates obtain their degrees by the "traditional" means of attending a college or university of their choice and taking a set of classes specific to their chosen field of study. While taking these classes, they are required to research a pre-chosen subject area, which they have developed under the supervision of doctoral educators. Upon completion of the research, the doctoral student is required to write a dissertation or thesis that presents the candidate's research findings. This document is submitted in support of a doctoral candidate's desire for a doctorate or professional qualification. After approval is obtained from a committee and the dean of the school of study, the doctoral degree is presented to the candidate.

The doctorate appeared first in medieval Europe as a license to teach. Its roots can even be traced back to the early church when the term "doctor" referred to the Apostles, the Church Fathers, and other Christian authorities who taught and interpreted the Bible. At the university level, doctoral training was a form of apprenticeship at a high level of training to which few were accepted. The usage and meaning of the doctorate has changed over time and is subject to both the cultural and regional influences of the country where the degree is to be conferred. Since the Middle Ages there have been considerable evolution and proliferation in the number and types of doctorates awarded throughout the world. A doctorate can have as many meanings as there are educational systems providing the specialized training. Several types of doctorates have evolved over the years; these can be classified into the following categories:

Research doctorates are conferred in recognition of academic research that is published in peer-referenced academic journals. Criteria vary throughout the world, but a near universal requirement is the submission of a significant body of original research undertaken by the candidate. This dissertation or thesis is examined by a committee selected by the school and the student, oftentimes requiring an oral examination in which the candidate appears before the committee members. The minimum time varies by country, school, and type of degree; it may be as short as three years or as long as ten years.

Higher doctorates are used in parts of the world to designate a higher tier of research doctorates. This doctoral degree is awarded on the basis of a body of published research (multiple research studies) by the candidate, who has done far more extensive work than just one research study. Higher doctorates are often awarded "*honoris causa*" when an academic institution wants to formally recognize an individual's achievements and contributions to a particular field.

Professional doctorates are awarded in certain fields in which most holders are not engaged in scholarly research, but in a profession such as law, medicine, and education. The term *professional doctorate* also refers to research doctorates where the field of study is used for professional purposes. These include doctor of education, business administration, management, theology, and others.

Honorary doctorates are awarded in formal recognition of an individual's achievement and contributions to a particular field or for philanthropic efforts. With an honorary doctorate the formal requirements of course study, research, and dissertation preparation are waived. Usually such doctorates are awarded to individuals who over a period of time have developed a body of work (such as in the arts or humanities) that is worthy of recognition. An honorary doctorate is based upon the discretion and criteria developed by individual universities or colleges; there is no "gold standard" by which these criteria are developed.

From Aristotle to the University of Somewhere

Early educational theory was defined by Aristotle, who existed before the birth of Christ and was known as the father of knowledge. Aristotle was a Greek philosopher who stressed the importance of education and stated that the individual man could learn to use his reason to arrive at virtue, happiness, and political harmony only through the process of education. This could certainly be true today in the United States where happiness is often tied to success. Happiness is defined as a state of well-being characterized by emotions ranging from contentment to intense joy. The happiness that Aristotle spoke of was not necessarily the same that one would think of having today. Today our view of happiness tends to be hedonistic. We want to feel good immediately and tend not to think too far ahead, so we see a night out or a pleasant activity as a route to happiness.

The ancient Greeks had a very different perspective on happiness. Aristotle spoke about achieving *eudemonia*, which may be roughly translated into happiness. *Eudemonia* is not an emotional state; it is more about being all that you can be, fulfilling your potential. The idea is that by living in a way that encourages us to reach our full potential, we bloom and flourish, and so display the best version of ourselves that we can be.

One can easily decipher from Aristotle's early works that in order to achieve a certain level of happiness, one needs an education to reach that goal. One's perspective of education may differ vastly from another's ideas of what is required to reach that goal. When one person decides to reach his or her full potential in education, the rewards are endless. Whether you choose to gain that knowledge through a technical school or from the University of Somewhere, it is a rewarding experience. Here in the United States the educational opportunities are endless, and there should be no lack of education to fulfill one's need and thirst for knowledge. As a student you need to choose the right opportunity that will best meet your individual needs and goals. For some that means stopping their education at a certain level, and for others that means choosing one program over another to fulfill specific requirements. For me, that meant finding a doctoral program in the field I wanted to study that would allow me to continue to work and support my family.

History of the Online Doctoral Education Model

The history of online education started much earlier than one would think. The first virtual classrooms were started in the 1960s when the University of Illinois created a classroom system with linked computer terminals. Students were able to access educational resources by listening to a professor's lectures that were brought in remotely by a form of television or other audio device.

By the mid-1980s a few online courses were emerging, and corporations were trimming their training budgets by introducing online tools to minimize software costs. As the digital age affected our nation, the first online school—the University of Phoenix, which was not accredited at the time—introduced courses to students via the computer. It was the fully accredited Jones International University in 1993 that really opened the world to the Mosaic Web interface and online education. Since that time, most standard universities and colleges obtained their accreditation and started offering online courses. Many now offer full degrees online, and the selection of degrees has expanded with time. What was once impossible is now possible: you have the ability to graduate with a degree of your choice without ever having to set foot in a classroom.

It appears that most online doctoral programs are aimed at individuals who want to pursue the program, but who choose not to quit their jobs. It is critical for students to recognize that this will take time away from their personal lives and at times from their work lives. Getting the degree becomes a great balancing act in which priorities need to be adjusted routinely to accommodate the time required for the doctoral program.

Before a decision is made regarding which school and program to select, several recommendations should be made. First, the student needs to determine whether the online program is from a virtual campus only or is connected to a brick-and-mortar institution. The latter usually has a wider base of support, including libraries and other infrastructures, and its high quality generally provides a better reputation for the degree. Second, the student needs to determine whether the school is fully accredited by a recognized accreditation organization. If not, you do not want to attend this college or university. Third, the student needs to be able to go on-site to meet with the advising professor on a regular basis, if possible, or if not to communicate regularly through telephone calls, online chat rooms, or emails. Fourth, the completion time to obtain a doctorate can vary widely. If the program advertises one year, then it is safe to assume that you do not want this program, as the degree may be worthless. Doctoral programs usually average 4 to 7 years to complete. Fifth, obtain all the information you can about the total cost for the doctorate. If the college with which you are working is hesitant to offer this information, that should be a red flag. The costs should include tuition, books, supplies, travel, software, taxes, and fees. Many courses require a residency component, so you should be able to obtain the entire estimated cost of these residencies, including hotel accommodations, meals, and travel expenses. Finally, you need to compare professors' experience, publications, and reputation. Your advisor will be the most important factor of your program. Make sure this individual is well respected and is experienced in helping doctoral students.

Other factors entering into your choice of which online doctoral program you choose will include whether you are self-motivated and have the ability to accomplish the amount of self-directed work you will be required to do. Find a group of people in your community who will support you. Often these are friends, relatives, colleagues, other doctors, and professional advisors within the community. This is not an easy road, so it is important that you have all of the support you can obtain. Finally, double check with current or potential employers to see if they will accept a credential from specific online doctoral programs once you obtain it. You do not want to put in all of the work just to be turned away from future positions and promotions. Keep in mind that some programs that previously had a poor reputation in the business community have greatly improved those programs and should now be given the same favor as other institutions of higher learning. It may take some effort on your part to educate the employer about the program. Many employers have no idea about the programs that are out there. Online education is a new idea to some, and it may take some adjustment for employers to begin to recognize online degree programs.

Types of Online Doctoral Programs

Several types of online education programs exist today throughout the United States, in which a person can obtain almost any kind of degree, from an associate to a doctorate. For the purposes of this discussion, I will focus on doctoral programs.

Hybrid Model – Online with Traditional "Ground" Classes

The hybrid model of online doctoral education can take on many different scenarios, depending upon the university. One institution may offer degrees in psychology and education while another may offer business management and health care administration. You need to review the offerings of the university you're considering to determine if it offers the coursework for obtaining the doctorate you desire.

The hybrid model includes online work with traditional on-campus courses. The connection with the university is stronger in terms of one-on-one contact, so your proximity to the university is crucial in allowing you the ability not only to attend the required on-campus courses, but also to meet with your advisor or counselor regularly. Some universities believe that the doctoral program, including the aspects of research and writing about the findings, would be incomplete without a face-to-face component.

Universities vary widely in administering campus instruction. Some require one campus course for every three online courses while others require less interaction.[12] Others require the student to attend one weekend of classes every month.[13] The hybrid model often gives the impression that the school is unwilling to let go of previous traditional methods of teaching and that it wants to play a larger role in the student's education. For some who need the face-to-face interaction, the hybrid model works as long as they have reasonable proximity to the school (see Chapter 2 for further discussion).

Online – With Ground Residencies

Most online doctoral programs have residency or colloquia requirements. Given that this is the most advanced degree you can earn, it's not surprising; earning an online doctoral degree is just as difficult as earning one on campus. However, not all online residency requirements are the same.

You may be required to visit campus only a few times a year for weekend seminars or meetings, or to attend a week of residency once a year, or to complete a full year of campus residency before distance learning begins. Online doctoral degree residency requirements tend to be non-negotiable, so you should know exactly what your doctoral program expects from students and should limit your potential choices to those with schedules that work for you.

The one-on-one contact with advisors or counselors is usually maintained by telephone, emails, and online postings. Once you know your advisor is online, it is very easy to simulate the give and take that comes from one-on-one contact. Most schools require the advisor to have a certain turnaround time, particularly during the period of the course.

All doctoral degrees require students to take specific courses. During the course you will be required to read provided materials and to develop feedback for your advisor and for the other students within your class, usually consisting of your ideas, thoughts, and opinions on the subject matter. These are presented as postings placed on a website that the entire class as well as the instructor can read. In preparation for writing your dissertation, you will often be required to write papers on the subject matter, frequently as a member of a team. The team often divides up the paper between the students, with each student being given a portion of the paper to write. Then the entire paper is compiled when all students have provided their portions. The requirements for the papers are usually governed by the same requirements the students will eventually encounter in writing their research dissertations following the completion of their research study.

The benefit of online learning with ground residence is that it gives the student much more independence to learn online and does not require as much face-to-face learning and on-campus requirements as the hybrid model does. It also gives the learner the benefit of residencies either quarterly or annually to check in with the university to ensure that students are on track and moving toward the completion of their doctorates. For those individuals struggling with their doctoral dissertation, the later residencies prove very effective in assisting those learners who are struggling for one reason or another.

Just as most of the learning for this model is conducted online, so are the studies, the statistical analysis of the study data, the writing of the doctoral dissertation, the defense of the dissertation, and the approval from the dean of the college. The classes and ground residencies prepare you for identifying what you would like to research for your dissertation. Your academic advisor should then approve your proposal, and you will choose your committee members. Once you have received initial approval for your proposal, you can conduct your research and begin writing your doctoral dissertation. Throughout the writing of the dissertation process you will be given significant support by your university, academic advisor, and committee members. Upon completing your dissertation, you will submit it to the university for approval. Once it is approved then you are ready to conduct your oral defense of the study you performed and its findings. When the oral defense is completed, the dissertation is submitted to the dean for approval. When the dean has approved it, you have earned your doctoral degree.

Entirely Online

As doctoral degree offerings have increased, some colleges offer the entire coursework, research, and dissertation writing online. This may sound quite foreign to those whose educational experience has been at traditional colleges or universities. But if you dread attending classes, the idea of an online education may sound very attractive. I believe you need to ask yourself if you want the educational experience or the degree. If you have already gained significant education by obtaining bachelor's and master's degrees and years of work experience, you probably have the educational experience and do not need to attend a college campus. If you want a degree, the idea of a totally online program is a means to an end.

Doctoral programs are tough, whether you are online or on campus. If you are the type of student who routinely needs the face-to-face counseling that you receive in class and in discussions with professors, then totally online education may not be the choice for you. With the totally online doctoral degree you never have to physically attend the school where you are enrolled. You do engage your teaching faculty throughout the online program, but it is not the same as meeting them in person.

With the online options you are required only to take the courses and complete the requirements of the program. This involves having a computer with adequate memory and the ability to access the Internet. I would also suggest a dedicated space within your home where you can sit down, close the door, and focus on your coursework. Once online and, of course, after you have paid or financed your tuition charges, you are ready to start. Some schools have specific start times and require that you begin at a certain level, while others require merely that you start a course at the first of each month. Another attribute that will help you with the online programs, particularly with online- with-residencies and totally online models, is the ability to get along well with others. Often you are assigned to a team of four to six classmates whose job it is to write portions of assigned papers. This activity will require you to be flexible, patient, and willing to accept another's point of view. If you are not a people person, you may struggle with this aspect.

Along with the coursework you will conduct your research and other parts of your doctoral study online, including writing the dissertation and gaining approval from your committee members and the university. These are individual activities that you do on your own with sometimes limited assistance from your academic advisor and committee members. I can say from experience that the rigors are just as great as working online with the hybrid model or online with the residencies, and even as rigorous as the doctorates obtained traditionally. You will learn a great deal and will be expected to apply the acquired knowledge throughout your area of study to include the defense of your dissertation. You will be challenged, perhaps more than by attending a traditional program at any university because of juggling your work, your family, and the demands of your doctoral program. As previously stated, most online doctoral students are still employed full-time in their existing positions. Despite the drawbacks, you will have the benefit of a doctorate degree at the end of the road, which runs anywhere from three to nine years.

Comparing the Traditional Model with the Online Model

In comparing the traditional model and online model, I have to draw from my college experience in obtaining a bachelor's degree at Trinity University in San Antonio, Texas, in the early 70s, and obtaining my master's degree from the University of Northern Colorado at the Air Force Academy in the mid-80s. One was strictly residential and allowed me to enjoy the full experience of college life, including my experiences as a football player. I went through my master's program when, as an Army officer, I was given the opportunity to attend classes at the Air Force Academy. Both gave me an example of what traditional education has to offer, and I will draw upon that experience in giving my thoughts on the pros and cons of traditional and online education. I will also draw on my experience of sending two of my four sons to college away from home.

Pro and Cons of the Traditional Model

The traditional model is that followed by most students who are beginning their post-secondary education. This is the time when one wants to leave home, get away from Mom and Dad, and start to develop as an adult. This is certainly something I can discuss with confidence, having attended a university 650 miles from my hometown. The student usually selects a school and is accepted for admission. Students are routinely assigned to dorm rooms with other students, whom they may or may not have met previously. The parents drop the student off at the dorm; this ritual of dropping the student off at college can be hard for both the student and the family as they begin their lives without seeing each other from day to day. A large percentage of parents have difficulty letting go, and for both the student and parents this can be very difficult. The social ability to get along with their roommate and other students in the dorm is a huge challenge for many students, who have come from their own rooms, in their own homes, and with their own ideas and habits.

Students in the traditional model are required to wake up on their own every day to make it to class and to make sure they are prepared. The students are responsible for showing up at a regular time on certain days and ensuring that they participate in class, study long hours, complete papers, and take tests when assigned. This type of schedule works really well for some people, and these are the people who are most successful. The class sizes can at times be overwhelming, depending upon the size of the school one selects.

The added benefit of the traditional model of schooling is the ready access to the professors and instructors in the assigned classes. Students have the advantage of listening to lectures and presentations in class and reinforcing the studying that they do in their off time. They also have the assistance of making appointments to meet with the professors or instructors to ask questions and to clarify any matters they do not understand. The universities also have the benefit of student tutoring or help centers, which often provide senior students to help students with classes that are difficult for them.

Students are responsible for budgeting their time and money to ensure that books are purchased, tuition is paid, meals and room rent are paid, and all of the other incidentals purchased that are necessary for living away from home for the first time. It is easy for students to let their budget get away from them when the impulse to buy is affected by peer pressure. Some students may feel overwhelmed with the combination of handling their own lives for the first time and keeping up with the demands of a large class load. The expectation is that the student will graduate at the end of four years, although realistically many students will take up to five years.

A large part of the traditional model of post-secondary education is the social component, which some may view as the attempt on the part of the university to "make up" for the fact that students' families live a distance away, even if it is only 50 miles. Students will often become extremely involved in the social part of college, which may include parties with no boundaries and exposure to new and different things. More often than not, during their first year of college students do not have a car to drive to school, and they are left to bicycle or bus around campus to make it to their classes on time. After the freshman year, if you live off campus, you are spending more money on travel, and you also could have to pay a nice price for a parking pass. My college parking was $90 per semester. Parking tickets can be approximately $15 if you happen to be on the wrong street on the wrong days. I used to park on a side street and then walk three blocks to school every day, which could be a big inconvenience. Not fun!

The campus experience can be worthwhile and something students will remember for the remainder of their lives, or it can be disastrous if the student parties too much and does not attend to the requirements of classes and living. If students have a healthy balance and remain committed to the primary reason they are away at college, which is to study and graduate, then they will do fine. Many students define themselves through their college experiences because college provides the first opportunity to grow up and to develop their own personalities away from parents and family. If they go into it with a positive, can-do attitude, they will usually succeed, but parents need to accept that some will not succeed. The traditional model of college is not the right fit for such students and young adults.

I reflect on the traditional model by first introducing the freshman experience because it is a springboard for discussing the traditional model for obtaining one's doctorate. The quest for the doctoral degree in a traditional school is parallel to completing a marathon race that requires extensive training, daunting endurance, and complete commitment to the process. I have always told others, when they have asked about the road to a doctorate, that it is not for the faint of heart. For most, the doctoral degree is the pinnacle of achievement and is not to be taken lightly. Obtaining a doctorate through the traditional method first requires that you determine what type of doctorate you want to obtain. Then you need to locate the university or college that offers this type of a doctorate. Once you have located the university that you wish to attend, the extensive application process begins. With the traditional model you are competing against other doctoral candidates who may or may not have more extensive backgrounds and higher undergraduate grade point averages than you do. The application process may also involve traveling to the university and engaging in interviews with the department head, professors, and potential mentors. The traditional model doctorates at universities are extremely competitive with only a handful being admitted to the programs. The requirements for obtaining a research doctorate entail successful completion of pertinent classes, acting as an instructor or research assistant in the area of your interest, passing a comprehensive examination, and defending a dissertation. Your professors want you to have the ability and stamina to stick through the process, including maneuvering through the competitive nature of professors, who are seeking ongoing funds and fighting the tenure battle. When you are finished, they will know what you are made of, based on your doctoral journey, and this provides them with a better assessment of how you will perform as a college professor.

I once had the opportunity to watch the work of a friend on her journey toward a doctorate at a Midwestern university. It required two years of coursework, which corresponded to the previously referred-to residency, while she taught a class of undergraduates every semester in the subject matter she was studying. The doctoral classes were on a strict schedule, much the same as for freshmen, so my friend had all of the pressures of getting up on time, being at class, including the transportation component, and then having ready access to the professors. Forget about working to earn extra money because most traditional doctoral students have very little time to do more than live and breathe their doctoral program. Then my friend was required to pass a series of comprehensive examinations, which were exhaustive and very difficult. Do you understand now that this is not for the faint of heart? Following completion of the examination the doctoral candidate was then required to conduct research and report her findings in the form of a dissertation. All of this work led up to the doctorate in her chosen field. My friend was very grateful for the work she had done, but exhausted by the intensity of the effort.

Pro and Cons of the Online Model

I can speak of this subject at great length since I researched the pros and cons of the online model of education to obtain my doctorate. The first issue that I had to take into consideration was that I was a full-time working professional who could not afford financially or professionally to take off work for 3-5 years. I also could not simply put my life on hold for 4 years to travel to a residential university to obtain my doctorate. I also had to consider my learning needs, professional priorities, and other personal circumstances in deciding whether the online model of doctoral education was right for me.

The benefits of the online model, first, are that the admission process, in some cases, may be less rigorous, thereby lacking the competition between peers. You are not tied down to when you have to go to bed or wake up for class. You never have to travel through a blizzard (as in my case) to get to class. And sadly, my school will hardly ever cancel classes even when the worst snow falls in Colorado, because it is sunny and warm in Phoenix. You can get a job and work the hours you want, and then during your free time, work on your school work. In addition to this, you can manage your own time and learn at your own pace. You spend no time commuting to a college campus and you have no additional travel costs for the trip. I was able to continue working my current job while taking classes. Your learning options are not limited by your geographic location: you can live in Washington and attend the University of Arizona. You can study when the kids are asleep or before work or whenever you need a good excuse to leave a party early.

If you prefer to write something rather than verbally express yourself to classmates and professors, then you may find online learning more effective for you. The instruction and coursework are highly customized to your field and subject, especially computer based training. You are able to use the office software, and at my university we were required to purchase a laptop if we did not have one. This is particularly important if you are traveling back and forth for quarterly or annual residencies for which you need a laptop for carrying your assignments along.

What is really nice about online learning is that you meet and work with classmates from the all over the United States and even from foreign countries. You usually meet them face-to-face during residency. In online discussions, no one person monopolizes the conversation, and 100% participation by everyone is required. Many times students are more vocal and involved in the discussion because it is online and they feel more comfortable stating their opinion than they normally would if it were face-to-face, so no more wallflowers. Several of the students with whom I attended had to skip a class because of work commitments or personal issues. They were able to make up the class at a later date with no problems. One of my classmates was from Hong Kong, another from Iraq, and another defended his dissertation from the submarine he was serving on at the time. I was attending classes during Hurricane Katrina, and one of my classmates was from New Orleans. He was able to take several months off to get his family settled into a new home. He then returned to New Orleans to help with the clean-up and to rebuild the levees, as he was employed by the U.S. Corp of Engineers, which was responsible for the levees' breaking. He returned to class at the same time he returned to New Orleans and was able to balance the commitments.

Although you do not necessarily have to spend money on hard copy textbooks, you will likely have to pay electronic resource fees and spend the money on computer upgrades and an Internet connection. I can be a visual learner as much as an auditory learner, so I would frequently take notes as I read the assigned reading online. Over time I found myself doing this less and less. It just made for an easier experience in learning for me all around. If I got home from work and was tired, I could choose to miss a day of engaging in the online discussions and get back to it the next day. Each class was followed by two reading weeks in which you could gather yourself together and get things done that you could not do during class, such as vacation, surgery, or the birth of a grandchild. It just made my online learning much easier when I had time in my schedule to take off. If you are returning to school after a period of absence, online learning allows you to continue your life with minimal disruption for schooling.

There are disadvantages to attending an online college. I think the primary disadvantage is not having the one-on-one face time with the instructors. Contact with instructors must occur either through emails, postings in the virtual classroom, or telephone calls. The nature of online learning requires that each student be participating 100% of the time. You are not left with the option to remain silent through one class; you have to post, engage in group discussions, and complete the written assignments, often with cooperation from your group.

This last requirement of the written assignments can at times be frustrating because if three group members are contributing to a paper and the fourth member is not contributing, it can be difficult. When we just could not get through to the fourth group member, we would turn it over to the instructor to address with that individual privately.

There is no question that your requirements for Internet access and the software needed could be an added expense to your household budget. You have to plan and adjust your schedule around assignment due dates. If a paper is due at midnight Mountain Standard Time, then you know you have to get it in early if you live on the West coast. You also need to know that because your cohort members are all in different time zones, you may not hear back from another student at the time you would like as that person may still be at work or in bed for the night. At times you can feel a sense of isolation or detachment from your school. I addressed this possibility by choosing a school that had local campuses so that if I felt that way, I could always just hang out at one of the school campuses. Frankly, I was so busy that I did not have time to hang out anywhere! I also thought I could use the library at these local campuses; however, the library contained online is so comprehensive that I never went to the library.

If you are an undisciplined individual, your attempt at an online education will have one of two outcomes: either you will become disciplined, or you will not succeed. You may forget you are in a class and forget to post, which I did on more than one occasion until I received an email from my academic advisor telling me I was in jeopardy of being dropped from the class. I started placing the class name and start date on my calendar to remind myself that I was starting a class on a certain date. It is also difficult at times if the school does not require you to have a textbook because everything is online. Nothing can be more boring for some students than staring at an eBook for an entire evening trying to focus and stay awake after working an 8-hour day. My solution for that was to print the eBooks, which wrought havoc with my budget from the costs of going through too much paper and too many printer cartridges.

Costs

Studies have shown that the costs associated with a doctoral degree are on the rise at a faster pace than those for other degree programs, including bachelor's and master's programs, across the United States. The cost of my doctoral program and how I would pay for it was very important to me. In determining the costs of a traditional program for a doctorate in Business Administration, I chose to survey three universities, one from each coast and a third from the

Midwest. For the online programs, I chose two well-known online programs and the third from a well known university in the state where I currently reside. What I found most interesting about this process was the various universities' positions in communicating the costs of their doctoral programs. Some were reticent to post the numbers for fear that potential candidates would shy away from the tuition, room, and board. Often doctoral candidates are responsible for their room and board and transportation, which translates to living in the economy and participating in the standard of living in that particular area. Many college towns see costs of living that are much higher than those in a similar size city or town without a college or university. Certainly the cost of living expenses affects your decision regarding the university you will attend.

At the eastern college I surveyed, the tuition ranged from $6,341 annually for in-state students to $11,231 annually for out-of-state students. Housing ran anywhere from $800 monthly for a studio apartment to $2,300 monthly for a three-bedroom family house. Most students are eligible for student aid through federal, state, and local programs, scholarships, grants, and other funding options specific for that school.

In the western college I surveyed, tuition ranged from $10,768 annually for in-state students to $25,809 annually for out-of-state students. Housing started at $1,000 per month for an unfurnished one bedroom apartment in a high-cost district. At the Midwestern college I surveyed, tuition ranged from $31,906 annually for in-state students to $45,172 annually for out-of-state students. Housing started at $454 per month for an unfurnished, one-bedroom apartment in a low-cost area and went up from there—quite a bargain compared to housing on either coast of the United States.

With the online program I investigated there was no differentiation between in- and out-of-state tuition for a doctoral program online. This university set the tuition and costs at $48,000, and that was it as long as you did not have to repeat a course or extend your dissertation beyond 4 years. For each year you remain a student while writing your dissertation beyond the 4 years, you are required to continue to engage in a class which costs $1,200 every 2 months, plus the residency fee of $2,400. So it could get quite costly if you had to extend your graduation due to problems with writing the dissertation or other issues.

The second online program I investigated charged $3,990 per quarter which amounts to $47,880 for the entire doctoral program (4 quarters x 3 years). The costs and other fees equaled about $2,000, so this is similar to the first program I surveyed. I should note that these are the two programs I considered extensively when preparing to begin my doctorate.

The third online program I surveyed was from a university located in my home state of Colorado. The reason I thought it was important to survey one online program that had grown out of a previously traditional program was to demonstrate the extent to which these programs are evolving throughout the United States. It appears that previously traditional programs are beginning to recognize the value of online programs in generating a larger student caseload, particularly among established professionals out in the workplace who desire to return to school to enhance their skills and ability to advance in their organizations. The doctoral program that I previewed was different from the one in Business Administration. In this case, it was one of only two online programs offered at this time and was in College and Educational Leadership, which includes education classes and human resources classes. The cost of this doctoral program is $625.00 per credit hour for a 60-credit course load, along with miscellaneous fees; together everything adds up to about $25,000. It is clear from reviewing the particular university's offerings that its online doctoral programs are very limited at this time. Hopefully, with time the offerings will expand and will draw a stronger base of support.

Time to Completion

How long your doctorate takes depends on what type of doctorate you are receiving and what school you are attending. An online doctoral course requires somewhere from 9 to 12 hours per week. A traditional doctoral course requires carrying a full load of classes, much like attending a traditional college for 2 years. Following that time, the student will commit 30-40 hours per week for the next 2-3 years or however long it takes to complete the doctoral requirements. I have seen students complete their doctorates in 4 years, and some take 6 to 7 years. Much is dependent upon your commitment to staying on task, to avoiding interruptions and other obstacles, and to being very focused.

Personal Experiences

My desire to obtain a doctorate was based upon the dreams of a young man from a tiny New Mexico village who, upon graduation from high school, was told that he would never obtain even a C in any college class. I saw the small village where I lived to be limiting, and I recognized that the only opportunity available to me was to graduate from high school and, with my football abilities, earn a scholarship to a university. The adults around me discouraged me because so many had failed. I took that as a challenge and, with my C average, went on to a reputable and high-ranking academic university in Texas to play football and, oh yes, earn a degree. This opportunity opened many other doors for me as I soon recognized that my focus had to be on my education and not on my skills on the football field. By embracing the teachings at that university, I began to excel, and this laid the groundwork for my pursuit of a master's degree and then a doctorate.

As I look back over my experience, I recognize that I was a very fortunate person. I saw many of my former classmates attempt to go to college and, lacking my athletic experience, drop out either because of their poor preparation from a substandard educational system, from lack of finances to support their effort, from homesickness, or from basic discouragement. As I continued my educational experience, I was exposed to a variety of opportunities, both in the military and in the civilian sector. Whether in Air War College or in a master's program at a university, I found that my commitment to education vastly enhanced my continued thirst for knowledge and my level of happiness. I believed I had the "right stuff," which was further demonstrated by my successful military career as an Army officer. As my second career developed in the civilian sector, I repeatedly began to ask questions about different business processes and procedures and the human factor, for which there appeared to be limited scientific knowledge.

Having the knowledge that I was a great manager and natural born leader, I believed that my effectiveness as a leader would be greatly enhanced if I were to complete a doctoral program in management. For me, this was an excellent fit, and I embraced every doctoral course with intense curiosity and built upon my intelligence, creativity, and maturity. I was much like a flower blossoming in that with each course I continued to build upon that enthusiasm to learn more and to press the envelope, so to speak, in extending research in the management field. Many can espouse their beliefs in the management field. However, who can look to solid research and data to support their position?

I have provided you with this background to give you an idea of where I came from and how I was able to draw upon this experience. I would hope that you can compare your experiences with mine and can recognize that you too have potential, whether you come from a small town or a big city. This is the impetus that propelled me forward to reach toward the pinnacle of education in obtaining a doctorate.

When I sought out doctoral programs, there were none in the large metropolitan area where I resided. So I started searching online resources in anticipation of traveling 40-60 miles to obtain my doctorate. I determined that obtaining a doctorate in this state would require me to attend a traditional university, with two years of on-campus coursework, followed by two to three years of research, teaching, and then writing my dissertation. All of this would have required me to quit my job, spend extensive time traveling daily, and even the possibility of moving my family, all of which represented roadblocks for me. It was only after a significant amount of searching for 2-4 years that I decided to explore online possibilities.

I was given two or three online universities to explore for obtaining a doctorate. These were narrowed down by the degree options they offered, and I chose to go with one of two colleges that offered a doctorate of Management in Organizational Leadership. I was eventually attracted to one curriculum more than another. Of note, during the time I was seeking out a university, online options were extremely limited, unlike today where many programs are being offered online. I was able to confirm that the university I chose to attend was accredited through both a regional and independent accrediting organization. I was able to check the accreditation through a credible website.

What made the option that I chose most attractive was that this was an online program with annual residencies, which meant that I could continue my full-time employment while attending school. The big ticket item for me was having the resources available to fund this endeavor. This was accomplished by personal funds, financial aid, and other grants and scholarships. I did not hesitate to seek out funding sources from agencies related to my field of study and my background in the U.S. military. Today I would probably aim toward a less expensive program because too much education debt can be crippling.

I thoroughly enjoyed the learning style of reading eBooks, posting online, and getting feedback from other students and professors. Although I did not meet all of the students that I learned to know during the classes, I was able to define my cohort (group of fellow classmates) and we all connected at one level or another during the residencies. My cohort members identified with me when personal tragedy hit my family, when I underwent challenges that included the loss of a job, and particularly when we all started to write our doctoral dissertations. This was such a long and laborious process: we encountered many roadblocks and met the disapproval of parts and elements from our committees and from the university reviewers. At times we all wanted to run for the hills as we dug our way through the process; however, at the end we all felt that we had not only worked hard, but also had earned our degrees!

The questions many ask me are was it worth it, and would I do it again? The answers are yes and yes. I have reached the pinnacle of the education pyramid, and I am so very proud for having done that. My wealth of experience, coupled with my educational credentials, leads me to feel that I am an expert in the field of management and organizational leadership. In a real sense I have reached Aristotle's goal of virtue, happiness, and political harmony only through the process of education. As an added benefit, I do so enjoy the new title I hold of Doctor!

Chapter 2: Asynchronous Communication

Cheryl Szyarto

It was less than 15 years ago—October 1996, to be exact. I can remember quite vividly that it was a bright, brisk day in the Northeast on a bustling college campus at the city limits of Scranton, Pennsylvania. The warm sun shone brightly upon me that morning, its external energy matching the unmistakable sensation within. I felt my insides glowing as I grew increasingly comfortable and confident with my newfound independence, an independence that would become more defined over the course of my 15-year academic journey. The scent of freedom, as I then knew it, was downright invigorating just as was the fresh, cool air gently brushing across my face and through my hair. It was my freshman year of college.

The walk from my dorm room to the campus library was a long one, but with great pride I traversed the campus with my head up and shoulders back. The walk would become familiar—one I would take morning, noon, and night as both a student and a circulation desk worker. On this particular afternoon, with several large textbooks and notebooks in tow, I marched toward the campus library in full student mode. As I approached the main door, I remembered to follow the strict no-food-or-drink-allowed policy and tossed my disposable coffee cup, still half full with my late morning joe, into the nearby trash receptacle. I then whisked out my stack of 50 or 60 3-by-5 note cards, skillfully covered (front and back) with important facts to study from early American history. I was headed to the fourth floor, through the double doors, past the front desk, down the corridor to the elevator, and up a mere three levels from the main entrance to the study lounge. Today, though, was different.

What in the world was the reason for that line? A somewhat orderly group of students was waiting patiently for a turn in the computer lab. There was a line outside of the computer lab? It was only the third or so week of classes—maybe the fourth. Were students already faced with pressing assignment deadlines? Lengthy papers to be typed and printed? Not one of them held a computer disc (yes, I said computer disc), no texts, notebooks, or papers in tow. Looking for any good reason to delay my independent study session, I curiously ambled on over to the line outside of the computer lab.

"What's going on?" I asked a familiar face at the end of the line, "Why the long wait for a computer today?" With a slight grin on her preoccupied face, the fellow student responded, "Oh, we're here to set up our email accounts." Oh right, I thought, email. I've been meaning to see what that email business was all about since I'd heard about it in new student orientation a month or so back. With that dreadful history quiz weighing on my mind, I figured now was the perfect time for a distraction. A 30-minute wait or so later, I was punching out my first email to a high school friend on a college campus 57 miles away. Best of all—it was easy AND it was free!

At that very moment, technology graciously entered my life. Communication with friends and loved ones became so much more convenient. Why had I not explored email a bit sooner? If only my boyfriend at the time (now husband) had had email access on his military base, I would not have spent countless hours in between classes or on lonely nights in my dorm room waiting by the phone for his possible calls. Likewise, I could have given up the wait for snail-mail deliveries, which just seemed to feel longer and longer as that first year of college passed. On that day, that memorable fall afternoon in 1996, I redefined my interpretation of personal freedom and independence. One college transfer and two degree programs later, computer technology had assumed a greater presence in my personal and academic lives.

However, the greatest change of all to my definitions of freedom and independence came in July of 2003—only 7 years after my introduction to email communication in my freshman year of college. Using my husband's past experiences as a full-time online student and military serviceman as a guide, I investigated online education with great enthusiasm. I was ready to embark on my journey as a doctoral student. Yet, as a full-time educator, homeowner, and new wife with a career-driven husband and plans to begin a family on the horizon, revisiting a traditional college campus was just not a practical choice for me. While I would never underestimate the value of my traditional brick-and-mortar school experiences nor the social, emotional, and academic growth and development such experiences had promoted, I clearly understood (despite how clichéd it might sound) that there is an appropriate time and place for everything. Full-time or even part-time on-ground classes would not be feasible for me. Yet, I could not put my dream to earn my doctoral degree to rest. Instead, my definitions of freedom and independence needed to evolve once again. Online, distance education was the answer. With the asynchronous nature of online education, the student (a.k.a. parent, spouse, employee, community volunteer, etc.) can, with greater control, define a personally appropriate time and place for academic goal achievement in spite of existing work, home, and familial obligations. I had found my path!

Definition and Instructional Qualities of Asynchronous Learning Networks (ALNs)

Not to be confused with synchronous e-learning, asynchronous learning involves the use of online learning resources, but is not limited by the constraints of time and place. With constructivist roots and, hence, a strong emphasis on student-centeredness, asynchronous learning is a teaching method that allows educators to facilitate learning among networks of learners who are separated by physical space and time. It is not uncommon for online distance education classrooms to accommodate students nationwide, and in many cases, worldwide.

Ideally, instruction in the asynchronous, virtual classroom differs from instruction in typical brick-and-mortar classrooms. If asynchronous learning is to be effective, instructors in asynchronous virtual classrooms must alter their affective, cognitive, and managerial roles and behaviors to best reach students and engage them in higher-order learning.

A meaningful affective relationship between students and instructors in the asynchronous virtual classroom is achieved through exploration of and engagement in alternate forms of emotional expression, and through the thoughtful and explicit communication of intricate thoughts and ideas. In my experience as an online learner, I always found it fascinating how instructors would skillfully diffuse heated and emotionally charged course discussions, redirect tangential discussions, and convey passion for content in the virtual classroom. With the absence of face-to-face contact and, therefore, the loss of nonverbal communication, my online instructors indirectly modeled and trained my fellow cohort members and me how to communicate personal feelings and beliefs skillfully and tactfully, as well as how to construct well-structured content-driven arguments in the written form. The applicability and transference of such skills to my professional life have been tremendous.

The cognitive and managerial roles instructors play in asynchronous online classrooms are equally important to their affective roles. With the loss of spontaneous follow-up questioning to seek clarity and the absence of instantaneous feedback in asynchronous learning environments, instructors are faced with the challenge of digging deeper into content matter. They must engage cognitively with course content in order to pose more probing questions and, thereby, strategically elevate the complexity of course discussions. The need for such instructors to craft more explicitly defined assignments and grading rubrics is also apparent in the absence of extemporaneous question-and-answer periods common in the traditional classroom.

In my first series of online courses, I was amazed at how much more challenging I found routine discussion questions to be and how much more effort was necessary to show mastery of course content; no longer would it be possible to ride on the coattails of the more verbal classmates in the traditional setting. Yes, my instructors always facilitated and emphasized the value of collaboration with peers; however, to ensure individual student understanding of content, instructors reliably monitored the degree of substantive involvement from each student on a daily basis. Long gone were the days of dozing off in the back of a crowded lecture hall or getting by with simply showing up for the midterm and final exams. With every written word archived in the online learning forum, instructors evaluated and held me accountable for my every word (or lack thereof). Indeed, I was getting my money's worth!

Advantages

My definitions of student freedom and independence continually evolved over the course of 15 years. I can honestly say that the greatest advantage of asynchronous learning in the online classroom is synonymous with my latest definition of student freedom and independence: "anytime, anywhere" education.

Asynchronous learning using online learning resources has enabled me to fulfill my desire to be a devoted wife, hardworking career woman, and dedicated mother while still being a full-time and committed lifelong learner. Granted, I have had to tame my Type-A personality and allow myself to indulge in one role more than in the others at the necessary times. Though I routinely needed to reassess my time management and ability to strike a personal, professional, and academic balance, the opportunity to fulfill my desire of earning a doctoral degree at this stage of my life was within reach, thanks to the nature of asynchronous, online learning— and, of course, the support of my close friends and loved ones. With each passing class, I saw my motivation, retention, and learning productivity increase.

The advantages of asynchronous online learning are not limited to factors related strictly to the freedom and flexibility it affords in one's life. In fact, one of the most wonderful advantages of asynchronous online learning is having the ability to share ideas and to collaborate daily with students worldwide.

Whereas my freshman year study group at the Jesuit university I attended on the east coast typically consisted of three or four students of like age, background, and experience, the study groups and learning teams with which I engaged during my asynchronous, online doctoral studies were heterogeneous in nature. They were most often comprised of individuals logging in from all over the United States, as well as overseas locations. Due in part to great variances in age, cultural background, and professional experience, group discussions proved to be more enriching and, thus, much more valuable.

The asynchronous learning environment is also ideal for students wishing to participate actively without the external pressures associated with extemporaneous speaking. Provided students use proper netiquette (see related tips below), thoughtful, lengthy, research-based answers in the asynchronous online environment can replace the hasty responses often shared in a face-to-face setting, where students may feel pressured to contribute or may be called upon to speak unexpectedly.

Likewise, students can conveniently avoid the possible frustrations associated with behaviors typically evident in traditional classrooms, such as classroom discussion domination or interruptions by one or more students. What is more, learners can participate in various discussion threads simultaneously without disrupting the general flow of discussions in progress. In other words, learners in asynchronous virtual classrooms can weave in and out of discussions, satisfying the need to pursue tangential paths of questioning, without interfering with participants' concentration on the central course topics.

Finally, one often overlooked benefit of asynchronous online communication is that student and instructor input is archived for later access. With the ability to reference discussion transcripts at a later date, learners can revisit past discussion topics in which they were, or were not, active participants. Learners can also save and organize discussion material for use in future courses of study and use the transcribed material to assist with reports or related post-discussion assignments.

Challenges

Of course, challenges associated with asynchronous learning do exist, yet they vary in degree, depending on students' skills and dispositions. If you are relatively unfamiliar with technology or are uncomfortable using technology as your primary medium of communication and learning, you may find the asynchronous online classroom challenging initially. The reliability of hardware and software can influence the accessibility of the learning environment; however, reputable online universities will provide students with 24-hour technical support from qualified individuals whose primary goal is to facilitate your learning experience and rectify technical difficulties to the greatest extent possible.

As a student in an asynchronous online classroom, I found the occasional technical glitch to be much less frustrating than the more frequent bouts I would have in traffic on the hectic, rush-hour commute to my ground campus as a traditional graduate student. Traffic delays, parking tickets, and inclement weather conditions were routine frustrations with which I had to contend as a traditional student, not to mention that addressing a student-related dilemma most often required a lengthy commute between buildings or campuses. In the asynchronous online environment, help is always a phone call or an email away.

While the asynchronous learning environment has its advantages, it may pose challenges for individuals who struggle with written communication methods and related skills in the online forum, such as typing and interpretation. Likewise, some students may find it challenging to cope with the delayed response time characteristic of asynchronous communication methods.

Related Tips

Given the aforementioned challenges and my personal experiences managing them, the following list of tips should prove helpful to learners who are considering advanced degree study in an asynchronous online environment:

- Ensure that your system meets the minimum technology requirements; install no fewer than the required software programs.

- Limit accessibility frustrations by noting and working strategically around the university's routine "downtimes" for systems maintenance.

- Abide by generally accepted communication behaviors online; use netiquette.

- Be cognizant of cultural diversity and individual differences, which may affect students' communication styles in the asynchronous online forum.

- Seek regular facilitator and peer feedback regarding your communication style and methods to ensure you are meeting discussion requirements timely and effectively.

- Research and, if appropriate, use assistive technology devices to cater to your individual learning style. For example, text-to-speech software may prove useful to auditory learners.

- Regularly take advantage of student workshops offered asynchronously through your university to improve your comfort level with the online classroom.

- Become familiar with the student support services offered online through your university (e.g., tutoring services, writing support centers, etc.).
- Given the need for self-discipline in the asynchronous learning environment, create a time management plan to ensure a balance between your personal, professional, and academic lives.

Leadership Connections

Today certain technologies enable students and professionals to engage and collaborate in ways not formerly possible. Distance learners in asynchronous learning environments have the opportunity to develop and refine leadership skills desirable in present-day workplaces. Such skills include, but are not limited to, effective written communication, time management, and coordination of geographically and temporally dispersed resources.

The interactive nature of communication in asynchronous distance learning classrooms reflects the basis of project-based work in 21st century business enterprises and educational institutions where geographically and temporally dispersed networks of individuals can establish and collectively work toward fulfilling organizational missions. Individuals with asynchronous online learning experience at the doctoral level are honing the leadership skills necessary for succeeding in today's fast-paced, technology-driven workplace.

Chapter 3: Is Online Learning For Me?

Andy Elliott

"Dr. Elliott, didn't you earn an online doctoral degree?" asked one of my graduate students before our class began one evening.

"Yes, I did receive my doctoral degree through an online university, and I am really proud of that fact," I answered, wondering where this conversation was leading.

"Can I do it? What I mean is—how do I know if an online learning environment is for me?"

This conversation has occurred many times since I received my doctoral degree. People are curious and want to know if the avenue I chose will work for them. Since I often hear these questions from prospective doctoral and graduate students, I began to create a series of questions that would assist individuals in determining if the online environment suited them. If they answer "yes" to the questions, then I can soundly recommend an online environment. Some of them may seem silly and others may seem serious, but a "yes" answer will ensure you are in the right venue. A list of those questions and a general discussion of expectations are as follows:

1. Do you know how to operate your computer and the various programs needed for success like MS Word® and PowerPoint®?

2. Are you able to communicate your ideas, intentions, and needs through the use of a written medium? Do you understand the difference between formal and informal conversation?

3. Are you willing to ask for help if you need it?

4. Do you have the time (15 hours weekly at a minimum) to devote to an online learning environment?

5. Do you have strong reading and writing skills?

6. Are you self-motivated?

7. Do you understand the importance of critical thinking skills?

8. Do you love to learn?

9. Do you work well with others?

10. Do you enjoy a challenge?

Discussion #1 - Technology

Knowledge and application of technology will be an immense help to you as you learn in the online world. Before you even consider an online program, you should be familiar with Microsoft Word, PowerPoint, Excel, and Adobe Reader. Each of these applications is used extensively during the online program. Some universities and even local libraries offer free introductory or refresher classes. If you are unfamiliar with any one of the aforementioned applications, you have some work to do before moving on to the next discussion. Also, familiarize yourself with the various search engines, online libraries, chat rooms, and email accounts that would maximize your online learning experience.

Discussion #2 - Communication

Communication is imperative. We have all heard that if we talk the talk, we'd better be able to walk the walk. An effective leader (which is what you are if you are considering a doctoral degree) must make full use of the power of language. I have discovered my own "Cs" that I need for effective communication. They are even more imperative in the online environment:

1. Clarity – A prospective leader must be sure the message is clear and understood by all his constituents. You need to understand that there is a time for informal discussions (as we are having here) and formal discussions (which will be when you write your papers). Be sure that your spelling and

grammar are clear and distinct so as to not distort your message in this environment.

2. Consistency – A leader must communicate on a regular basis. His message should be consistent within the organization. Through your online communication you send a message: "I can be relied on; I am regularly involved; I respond to others' comments or questions within a reasonable amount of time."

3. Constructive – A leader needs to be constructive in the advice given to others within the organization. Leaders must ask themselves if this advice is going to help or hurt others. Constructive criticism may be necessary, but the key is for the feedback to be tactful. When given constructively, feedback involves tact and will not hinder the organization. This is where your tone is crucial in the online world. Be sure to re-read everything that you write before sending it. The tone needs to be considerate and cautious, not curt and crass.

4. Collaborative – Communication within any organization (especially the online world) should be collaborative. The leader must encourage others to share their ideas and opinions. He or she must constantly involve colleagues in the decision-making process. This keeps the organization

going in multiple directions. It also helps to know others are on your side.

Discussion #3 - Asking for Help!

I have often been asked by my wife, children, and close friends why I never stop and ask for directions. My pride, my nature, or perhaps my innate ability to rely on the sun, moon, and stars for assistance has kept me from seeking help. An online doctoral program is not like that at all. In fact, if I had not swallowed my pride very early on in this program, I would not have succeeded.

Countless times I found myself asking for help. I would ask my teacher for assistance if there was confusion with an assignment; I would ask my colleagues to edit or review material; I would ask technical support over the phone to help me solve problems; I would ask my friends and co-workers for prayers and patience; and I would ask my wife and children to understand when I could not make it to all the family functions or sporting events.

Without help in this program, you will not succeed! So....ask for it in advance, and it will be there when you need it!

Discussion #4 - Do I Have the Time?

Many individuals will quit their full-time jobs to pursue a doctoral degree, and they still struggle for time. That said, I do not advocate that you quit any job or give up on anything. I do, however, think it is essential to improve your time management. If you properly manage your time, an online doctoral program is very doable!

As a student, expect to spend 15 hours a week in class discussing, researching, and writing. That may be too much time for some of you and not enough for others. Time is something that needs to be gauged as soon as you begin the program. It is fair to say that everyone has a path that works best for him or her. I learned to balance my time early on (see the "Personal Experience" section at the end of this chapter for a little example of what my day looked like—not to brag or scare you away, but to remind you that if I could do this, you can do it too!).

Discussion # 5 - Abilities

Everyone knows his or her own ability levels. I would strongly advise that you have the ability to read well, write prolifically, and communicate skillfully with several people at a time. This type of program is truly for one who is familiar with multi-tasking. There will be times when you are reading, writing, and speaking at the same time. Someone once said that a program such as this requires an individual to exhibit ADHD, or the tendency to be *actively devoted and highly dedicated*. This, in turn, has given us a great segue to move to the next discussion.

Discussion #6 - Learning Style

As an actively devoted and highly dedicated doctoral student, you need to be self-motivated. I encountered several individuals that dropped out of the program for lack of support. Were there times when I felt alone? Yes! Were there times when I was discouraged? Yes!

Yet, I reminded myself that the only person who can change me is ME! It is essential to stay motivated. You can do this! It all comes down to how much you really want to be a doctor. Well, for me I could all but taste the title and the opportunities that called my name! In retrospect, it was all worth it! Walt Disney once said, "The way to get started is to stop talking and begin doing."

Obviously, the answers to the remaining questions are easily answered. If you can think critically, love to learn, work well with others, and enjoy a challenge – there is only one thing left to ask: What are you waiting for?

Personal Experience: One Day in My Life as a Doctoral Student

One morning not so long ago, I was up at 5:00 a.m. I did the normal things: showered, shaved, took the dogs out, taught an on-line class, woke up the children, and grabbed a bite to eat. I was gone by 6:30 a.m. with my youngest son in tow (at this time he still went to school with Dad). I stopped at the grocery store to pick up some last minute items for a school science lesson and was at school by 7:15 a.m. If you teach, you understand that the moment you reach school until you leave, your life is not your own. To add to the confusion, the principal was gone, and I am the acting administrative designee. So...I got to perform two jobs with a class full of students. School ended at 2:30 p.m. I taught an afterschool GATE class until 4:00 p.m. I drove 45 miles to teach an on-ground class that lasted until 10:00 p.m. I came home, checked my online class, answered student questions, and made a few posts. Then I switched gears; I became the student and completed the work for my online doctoral class. I answered questions, made a few posts, wrote down some research notes, and signed off at 12:30 a.m. My day was done! Uh-oh—I forgot to let the dogs out!

Chapter 4: Is There Time For Me?

Leilani Longa

"If time be of all things most precious, wasting time must be the greatest prodigality, since lost time is never found again."

- Benjamin Franklin

Time means different things to different people. Some people look at time as a moment or an occasion, while others look at time as a period or duration; either way, something, somewhere, is taking place; a non-spatial continuum is measured in terms of events that succeed one another from past through present to future; or it may be the point or period when something occurs. No single meaning or explanation of time will be encountered the same way, nor will all individuals manage it similarly. Managing time involves a personal learning process of discovery and exploration of what works, what does not work, and what can be changed or adjusted to make time.

This chapter provides insight and information on how time is spent in a day in the life of a doctoral student. Several aspects must be considered when one makes a decision to embark on the doctoral journey. This chapter explains the importance of knowing oneself in relation to time, the ability to balance everyday life in harmony, the skill and talent of time management, planning, and organization, as well as the commitment to the time it takes to achieve the goal of becoming a doctoral scholar. The task of managing time may be arduous, and the work may be tedious; but understanding the significance of time in the beginning contributes to making the voyage more endurable in the end.

Personal Awareness

"Do not squander time for that is the stuff life is made of."

- Benjamin Franklin

Personal awareness is self-awareness, which is the ability to know and understand one's self and the conscious knowledge of one's own character, feelings, motives, and desires. In being personally aware, one demonstrates actions that contribute to effective interaction with oneself and others. Knowing and understanding one's own habits, behaviors, and lifestyle is essential to knowing if there is time in one's life to complete the doctoral journey. Are you a planner or are you a procrastinator? Do you need peace and quiet to work, or do you need music and the television to be humming in the background? Are you a multitasking worker who is able to engage in multiple tasks simultaneously, or are you a more linear, focused, concentrated worker? Having an awareness of what type of person you are is significant.

Understanding How You Spend Your Time (Current State)

Understanding how time is spent in your daily life is fundamental. Before starting a doctoral program, you must think about several competing items. Think about how you spend your time. How much time do you spend at work? How much time do you spend at home? How much time do you spend at school? It is also critical to list other ways that you spend your time aside from work, home, and school. These topics will be discussed in more detail in the following section.

Making a list is a basic step and an essential key to success. Did you ever conduct a time study on yourself? For this chapter, your job is to understand how you use time. The elements in your list should consist of the following main categories: work, home, school, and other. Capture the amount of time you spend doing certain tasks such as washing dishes, watching television, driving, sleeping, working, and all the tasks you perform on a daily basis. Writing out daily tasks will help you identify pockets or windows of time to spend toward researching and writing your dissertation, as well as participating in the overall doctoral program. As you analyze the data you gather during your personal time study, you will need to make some agreements and compromises with yourself. It is up to you to decide how long you plan to stay in your program and complete your dissertation. The university will allow some students to take 3 ½ to 5 years to complete their course work and dissertation. This timeline varies by university, of course, with some permitting longer windows of time. The information list and time study data you analyze provide a baseline for how you spend time in your daily life.

Knowing How You Want to Spend Your Time (Desired State)

After you have completed your analysis and once you have made some agreements and compromises with yourself, it is time to make some decisions on your desired state. Knowing how you want to spend your time is important because you can begin setting time aside to incorporate the doctoral program and dissertation process into your daily routine. The future state is a part of your value stream mapping. Value stream mapping is a Lean tool used in manufacturing. The concept is used in manufacturing to map out a current state with an eye to improving toward a desired or future state that is more efficient. The goal is to assess the current state and draw a future state describing every activity involved to get to your desired state. Once you have mapped out your desired state of time, you can work toward this new state of expectation. Identify how much time you will spend researching and writing your dissertation while managing all of the other areas of your life.

In the beginning, this is not easy to do. It takes practice and a change of habits. You will find that you have conflict within yourself whether you should attend your best friend's house-warming party, complete an assignment, or turn in a draft of a dissertation chapter by the assigned deadline. Changing your habits requires a change in behavior. When you change your behavior, you are making a conscious decision and taking action for this new lifestyle adjustment. If you were once a procrastinator and enjoyed doing things at the last minute, this may not be an ideal situation for you. Once again, that is why it is so important to know yourself and to have self-awareness.

A Balancing Act

"Take time for all things."

- Benjamin Franklin

One thing you will learn during your doctoral studies is how to balance work life, home life, and school life. This is not easy, and some students find it quite challenging, especially if they are caring for children or elderly family. The demands are enormous for one person, and then to decide to take on another set of responsibilities could possibly drive you insane. The saving grace for most students is the level of support, encouragement, and understanding they receive from others in their lives who are there for them while they venture into the new world of academia. I always tell myself and others to stop regularly and smell the roses, and to celebrate milestones, no matter how great or small. Make time with bosses and coworkers, family, and instructors to check in and get their perspectives and feedback on how things are going as you move through this journey. Once again, it is not easy to add more responsibility to an already full plate. Also, having the ability to take deep breaths, take a time out, and meditate during stressful times is important. Sometimes you need an escape that others may not understand at the time, but setting expectations and sharing your experience with others may help ease tension in an already tense and sensitive situation.

Work Life

Sometimes people choose to set out on the doctoral journey for career advancement. At times, this is easy to discuss with your employer and co-workers; other times it may be a difficult discussion that could cause conflict in the workplace. Whether or not you choose to share your plans with others is up to you. One constant is that if you have to work during your doctoral journey, it is important to balance this part of your life, especially if you are the bread winner in the family and job stability is important to you. One advantage can be the level of flexibility you have in your schedule, especially if you can gain some flexibility in your work. Such flexibility helps tremendously, especially when you have to meet deadlines on assignments. Also, take advantage of special programs that your employer may offer, such as a program that supports continuing adult education, which will allow you to take time off or have your education paid for by the organization. The option to receive paid time off or vacation from work is a great benefit as well, especially when it is time to attend any required residencies. In my doctoral program, year 1 residency was one week, year 2 residency was three days, and year 3 residency was one week. Optional week-long residencies in years 4 and 5 were made available for students in need of additional coaching or onsite mentoring. Having the ability to take time off from work to attend residency or focus on homework or writing papers and your dissertation is important. If you have a demanding job that requires 10 to 12 hours of your day, it may benefit you to have a chat with your employer to see if you can adjust your schedule, lower your level of responsibility, or get another position during this time. For some individuals this is not feasible, which can make life a little more stressful and overwhelming, and may cause burnout or illness. Negotiating a more manageable schedule at work will be highly rewarding while you are a doctoral student.

Home Life

Home life balance is somewhat like a teeter-totter. You have children, a spouse, parents, friends, family, PTA meetings, church, soccer, carpools, the family pet, neighbors, and time for you—if there is any to spare. If you find yourself struggling to balance work and family, you may need to reassess your time and decision to commit to a doctoral program and the associated dissertation research. Think about what a doctoral degree is worth to you. Are you willing to give up your work life and family life to complete your course work and dissertation? For most people, this would not be an option or a question. It is challenging to decide what to do, and the answer may not always be easy. To approach a discussion about home life balance, you are encouraged to collaborate with your loved ones and agree upon a decision that satisfies the needs of all parties. Proactively work together with your loved ones to understand each other's personal needs and the amount of time your doctoral studies may take away from them. Explain the sacrifice that it will take, as well as the support and help that you will need to make for a more harmonious transition. Providing them with as much information and realistic expectation up front as possible eliminates room for surprises and resentment down the road.

Also, it is helpful to make a list of chores around the house and to establish any agreements that need to be made prior to starting your doctoral program. Assess and access your resources; seek help from family, friends, or neighbors. If you are a parent, meet with your family to establish mutually agreed upon expectations for mommy or daddy time as well as school time and quiet time. Children should know what to do for emergencies or if they have questions or need an adult's input while not under your immediate supervision. Preparing breakfasts, lunches, and dinners in advance or chipping in with other household chores can be ways for your children to demonstrate their support of your academic endeavors. All modifications to household routines will need to be discussed and agreed upon by all parties in advance. You will need to periodically review the changes that everyone will experience and the importance of their working as a team. Support is very important during this time. The time study you created earlier will help to illustrate in which areas of your home life you will require assistance and support.

It is also a good idea to explain the positive outcomes that you may achieve after graduation. Talk about the benefits that will come after you complete your dissertation. As a parent, you can also talk with your children about the importance of continuing education, goal setting, and responsibility. In addition, remaining committed to spending quality time with your family is absolutely necessary. Do not set aside time only to talk about school arrangements and schedules; also talk about fun things, schedule family fun days, and plan engaging activities. If sitter arrangements are possible, commit to having regular date nights with your husband, partner, or significant other to keep the spark alive during the next few years. You may also want to talk about planning vacations. It is also essential to make time and take time for yourself. This will help you keep your sanity and keep you calm and balanced.

School Life

Balancing school life with your work and home lives is crucial to your success as a doctoral student. Your school life will be another responsibility to which you have committed, and the time analysis completed earlier will help in this area. You have already identified and carved out time that you can commit to school. Review your school schedule and your assignment workload, including participation in online discussions, any individual papers that you need to write, any team papers and projects on which you need to work, and of course time to research and write your dissertation. The aforementioned tasks and all other school-related responsibilities should be included in your time analysis and ultimately fit into the open pockets of time you have identified. Once again, knowing your habits and behaviors, as well as what you need to change, will become clearer as you balance all of the moving parts in your life. Identify clear roles and responsibilities with your professor or instructor and your learning team members. Understanding expectations up front with school helps you to be a better planner of your day and your time. Talk to others who are in your program or have been in your program so you can learn from the lessons that they have to share and the challenging road that they have successfully navigated.

In this new life, it is important for you to be flexible, adaptable, and versatile enough to move with the changing winds. If this type of lifestyle is new to you, it may take some adjustment for you, but ultimately it will help you and will minimize the times when things sneak up when you least expect it. You will be better prepared to handle and manage different situations in your work, home, and school life.

Managing Your Time

"Never leave that till tomorrow which you can do today."

- Benjamin Franklin

Have you identified what kind of time manager you are? Are you an on-the-fly spontaneous person or a planned person?

Do you write down lists or do you memorize what needs to be done? This is the time to get serious in developing a plan of action for approaching and tackling your dissertation. This is where your time management skills, prioritization, project management, and organization skills will need to take effect. Time management refers to skills, tools, and techniques used to manage time to accomplish specific goals.

Create a Plan

The first step is to create a plan. A dissertation is generally made up of five chapters; the Introduction, Literature Review, Methodology, Analysis, and Conclusions or Recommendations, along with appendices and bibliography. During the development of each chapter there are processes, which include selecting your mentor and dissertation committee members who will periodically review your work in progress, submitting to the university review board(s), finalizing your dissertation, completing the oral defense, and obtaining the dean's approval. The plan should include all of these major milestones as well as more detailed information on how to accomplish the ultimate goal of completing your dissertation and what needs to be prioritized, organized, and arranged to make it happen. The overarching plan can be a high level plan with a description of tasks, resources, and a timeline, which will be further discussed in the next section. Once your plan is created, review it with others to see if you have missed anything and to confirm if you are moving in the right direction.

Develop a Schedule/Timeline (Daily, Weekly, Monthly, Quarterly, Yearly)

Add a schedule or timeline with deadline dates to accomplish the milestones in the dissertation plan. Create daily, weekly, monthly, quarterly, and yearly accomplishments with details of what it will take to complete your dissertation. Share the categories, description, schedule, and timeline with your mentor, acquire an understanding of the plan, and establish any necessary agreements. The aforementioned tasks are important in helping to set clear expectations between you and your mentor. The parts of the plan that may take longer to work through than expected are residency schedules, your mentor and committee search and selection, dissertation reviews, changes, and approvals. Your control in such areas may be very limited because of others' availability or lack thereof, so their schedules may affect your dissertation plan. During this time, practice patience. The process can be long and grueling, but you will make it through if you remain committed and focused.

Prioritize Tasks and Projects

It is important to prioritize tasks and projects, as shared earlier. You will need to follow a specific process when writing chapters 1 through 5, as well as schedule time to conduct the study, analyze the gathered data, draw conclusions, and make appropriate recommendations. Additionally, there will be a continual back-and-forth process with the writing of each chapter along with continuous review, ongoing corrections, changes, and overall improvements within these chapters. You can expect to undergo rigorous processes, which include reviews with your mentor and committee, reviews with the university review boards, your oral defense, and the dean's review and approval process. Be certain to follow any required procedures related to documentation of edits and revisions. Give yourself a wide range of times for beginning and completing the aforementioned processes. Sometimes the experience may be frustrating and often conflicting between committee members, review boards, and the Dean. The strategy one should take to overcome the frustration is to be flexible in your plan and adjust as needed, move forward through the plan, and check off each of the deadlines and milestones as you complete them.

The 3 Ds

"You may delay, but time will not."

- Benjamin Franklin

Once you have determined that there is time for you, that you are able to balance work, home, and school life, and that you have created a promising action plan, it is time for you to work through it. You will encounter bumps in the road, but no hurdle along the way necessarily has to signify the end of your journey. Life will continue to happen as usual; however, the way you approach each encounter will make all the difference. There may and will be set backs; understand and accept that now. The road is not paved in gold, and life is not perfect when one is living in an unpredictable and complex world. However, there is a light at the end of the tunnel, and with focus and fortitude you will reach that light. When you enter the dissertation process, three significant concepts will be essential in achieving your goal: discipline, determination, and dedication.

Discipline

You must have self-discipline. Discipline is training to improve strength or self-control; to discipline thus means to instruct a person to follow a particular code of conduct. It is imperative to condition yourself in such a way so as to strengthen your mind, body, and spirit to accomplish the ultimate goal of becoming a doctoral scholar. Envision yourself as an ultimate fighter. You train and practice, day in and day out, to focus yourself on the goal, which is to be the champion. Conditioning and practicing every day helps you become better and better. You train yourself to remain focused on your goal, which might be writing a paper or completing your portion of a team assignment. You resist the urge to procrastinate or to be reactive instead of proactive. You must follow the mantra to be the best in what you do and to take your studies seriously. It is important for you to be disciplined as you prepare yourself to complete the doctoral program and dissertation. Discipline takes practice and repetition; you must have the ability to get up and dust off should you encounter interruption or defeat as you work toward your goal.

Determination

Determination is moving toward an outcome and devoting full strength and concentrated attention to it. The determination you have to accomplish your goal is a strong quality, and no one can stop you but you yourself. Making the decision to get a higher education at the doctoral level is the easy part; maintaining that inspiration and drive to keep going is the hard part. However, self determination is an admired and resilient quality for a doctoral student to have while on this journey.

Dedication

Dedication is a commitment to oneself to achieve the goal or purpose. Committing to achieving your goal is important. It is a level of devotion to yourself to give of yourself, to sacrifice something that is important to you. A doctoral degree is something that is well deserved, once earned. Attaining a doctoral degree results from hard work that no person can ever take away from you. Such a degree symbolizes the heart and perseverance to move forward continually toward your goal of becoming a respected scholar. It is imperative to stay focused on completing tasks and accomplishing what you set out to do. At this point, it is important to dedicate yourself to the attainment of a goal for which you have carved out time in your life to achieve and to accomplish something of which you and others will be proud. A doctoral degree is a mark of commitment and achievement in higher education.

Personal Experiences

Five years before starting my doctoral program, I had graduated with my master's degree. I told myself back then that in 5 years, if I am not in a job or career that makes my heart sing, I will go back to school and obtain my doctoral degree. Five years later, I was not in my dream job, nor was I on the right path to my ideal job. I made the conscious decision to return and continue my education as a doctoral student. Having been out of the game for a while, I was nervous and excited at the same time. I did not know what to expect of myself or of returning to university life. I researched several degree programs before I decided on a school to attend. I chose it because of its diversity and flexible programs, which cater to working adults. The university from which I received my bachelor's and master's degrees followed a similar value of encouraging diversity and accommodating working adults. This was something with which I was comfortable, and after meeting with one of the university's academic advisors, I knew this was the program for me. However, there was something new that added to my return to university life, and that was online classes and asynchronous learning. My previous university experience had been conducted on ground and in person, which I liked because I enjoyed the socialization process and collaboration with teams. I was not sure how I would fare in taking online classes, but I was willing to do it so that I could put myself on the right track to career and personal success.

Because I made a conscious decision to return to school and continue a higher education, I automatically placed myself back in school mode. Because I am disciplined by nature, it was not hard for me to create a plan for myself and to stick with it. The activities in my life were not difficult for me to rearrange. At the time, I was active in hula dancing and at my fitness center in kick boxing. I was in a new relationship. I was working full-time. My sister and brother and their families were the only other loved ones on the island where I lived. I received my doctoral program information, and I made a timeline of what I needed to do to accomplish my goal of obtaining my doctorate. I spoke with my significant other and my family and shared my decision with them. They knew that returning to school would take up a lot of my time. My siblings thought I was crazy, my parents were pleased, and my partner was happy for me that I was following my dream. Overall, I received full support from my family. Luckily, my director was very encouraging and understanding. He allowed me to work a flexible schedule and was extremely supportive of my choice to continue my education.

Because I knew I was in for a change in my daily life, I took a break from hula and kick boxing; however, I still continued my cardio workout by waking up early and exercising. I made time to focus on my studies for the next 3 ½ years. I was determined to follow through with my decision. Throughout the program I did miss several family gatherings, rarely spent excess time with friends, and minimized the number of times my partner and I went out. These changes, personally, were not hard for me to make, and that is because I had a very understanding support group made up of my family and friends. I must say, however, that when I did have a break from my studies, I squeezed in enough family and friends face- time to last until my next break. I also remembered to celebrate small accomplishments and milestones. My significant other and I would have little dinners or plan short getaways to celebrate. I really needed these types of things to help keep me going.

My experience may sound ideal; however, it was not all roses and rainbows. I experienced my share of frustration, doubt, and disappointment. During those times of despair, it was nice to have a shoulder to cry on to let me know that it was natural to take a break and regroup. My mom was key in easing my pain and making things all better, like when I would fall down when I was a little girl. She would pick me up, put a Band-Aid on my cut, wipe my tears, give me a kiss, and let me know that everything would be fine. I really needed that. My dad was so supportive by encouraging me to keep going and telling me that I was doing a good job. He knew that I was working hard to become successful in my personal life and professional career. My parents were both so proud of me, and I needed that reassurance to know that I could do it and accomplish my goal.

Chapter 5: Learning Teams—The Good, the Bad, and the Ugly

Ed S. Turner III and Leilani Longa

As I begin to look at teams in the dissertation process, I suppose readers are scratching their heads. This begs for an explanation. The dissertation process has one researcher completing the process alone. How do learning teams show up in this process? Learning teams are vehicles for collaborative learning in many online programs.

There are three separate occasions in which learning teams come into focus in the dissertation process. The first occurs when the student begins the doctoral journey and selects a field of study. The student is a member in a class of students pursuing a doctorate in the same field. The larger learning teams are often employed at required residencies. At each residency, the students within each program are dispersed so that each is exposed to different teams, and learning becomes more robust.

If enrolled at a university whose academic programs are designed around collaborative learning theory, students are also exposed to learning teams during each core course taken throughout their doctoral journey. The learning teams in such courses have the potential to promote opportunities for critical thinking and collaborative problem-solving. Typically the students completing courses together on the same team are from one particular group of the program, sharing experiences and exploring ideas.

The third opportunity to experience teamwork happens during the dissertation process when the researcher reaches the data collection phase. The organizational learning team may be used as means to retrieve data for collection and analysis.

Benefits of Learning Teams

Cohesive and productive learning teams can increase creativity and enhance problem-solving. If you listen closely to the discussions within a cohesive and productive team setting, most team members will demonstrate feelings of trust and empowerment. If a roadblock occurs, the members do not stop looking for a way to improve existing work conditions and improve the team communication internally and with the leadership team.

Challenges for Success

How does the learning team garner the support to function at a high level to influence team operation and enhance learning? This happens with the implementation of a team charter or operating agreement, which addresses operations when the team is united for the specific purpose of addressing a specific task, such as enhancing team operations or completing a formal assignment.

The learning team charter should contain the names of each team member, phone numbers, fax numbers, and email addresses. The key is to be able to remain in communication as the process moves forward.

Within the charter, each team member will enter his or her personal strengths and skills to assist in the delegation of tasks according to the members' areas of expertise. There may be specific areas in which a team member will want to develop his or her skills, in which case the team environment is an ideal setting to work toward the goal of self-improvement.

The charter should identify the goal(s) the team has formed to accomplish. As the development continues, each member should identify what barriers may block the success of the team. This process must be proactive and be geared toward eliminating barriers quickly.

The team members will need to agree upon ground rules for working together, which must include meeting schedules, locations, expectations, agenda formats, project completion and conflict resolution plans, and acceptable communication methods. Again, by creating a team charter, members will be proactive rather than reactive.

As previously noted, the charter must address the occurrence of conflict within the learning team. It should be understood that conflict is not something to avoid. The best solutions or communication can occur through conflict in a team. The charter should provide a plan to address conflict within the team setting to reach a solution based on collaboration.

It is usually helpful for leaders and members of learning teams to understand how newly formed teams move through developmental phases and how members can address the needs of the team during the evolution. Understanding the four stages of team formation can help to turn the team into a high performing team, making it more likely that each member will enjoy the involvement in a learning team and will grow personally and professionally by working in the team setting

Forming

During the forming stage of team development, the members get to know one another and begin to understand the assigned task for which the learning team was formed. The task for each team member is to begin to establish group norms and decide how to divide the duties to accomplish the tasks. Team members begin to test the leadership roles and to see how each individual fits into the team setting. There is little movement on task accomplishment in this stage since its prime purpose is for members to get to know one another.

Storming

During this stage of team development, the members begin to challenge the leader's role and to question the process chosen to accomplish the task the team has been given. If tension develops as communication styles evolve, conflict will emerge. If the conflict is handled successfully, the team can move on productively to complete the deliverables assigned. Otherwise, progress into the next phase can be thwarted.

Norming

In the norming stage the group faces issues, conflict, power, and leadership struggles openly and directly. Patterns of acceptable behavior emerge during the norming stage. Everyone has a role and understands how each member communicates and fits in the team. The team takes pride in being able to work out differences as they occur. If an individual does not help the team move forward, the entire team may regress to the storming stage until all team members feel comfortable in moving back into the norming stage. It is not uncommon for members to be at different stages of team development at any given time.

Performing

The performing stage of team development is the ideal level for the team. Here the focus is on the deliverables, and the team members really know one another. It is not uncommon for the members to begin to complete sentences for one another because they are so familiar with each other. The members are comfortable with and confident in the leader, in his or her style of communication, and in the model of leadership he or she uses to motivate and direct the team to attain its established goals.

Adjourning

The final stage in team development is adjourning. At this point, the team may have completed the assigned task and delivered the end-product on time. Team members may return to their assigned groups and there may be disappointment at having to close down the team. Typically the team will celebrate the accomplishment of the final task, consider the experience to be very positive, and be thankful for the team and the interaction between members.

My Personal Experience as a Learning Team Member

The learning teams established in each class and those formed during each residency support the doctoral students throughout the dissertation process. As a student in this process, I felt a great deal of pride in learning when each member of my learning team had received approval for his or her dissertation proposal from the university's Academic Review Board (ARB) and Institutional Review Board (IRB), and finally when each member had passed the oral defense for his or her dissertation. The journey was long and difficult, but each member of my cohort completed the process and grabbed the brass ring, attaining the Doctor of Management in Organizational Leadership. I became even more determined to complete my quest and attain my doctorate.

As I began the process of data collection, after receiving the go ahead from the IRB to collect data, I sent the email with the link to the validated survey to the study participants. In reality the participants became a learning team of sorts in that each felt trusted to offer input to improve the organization for which all the study participants served. The individuals of the unit cared about the results and trusted the leaders to take the data and work to improve the organization. This would add to the knowledge on trust and an organization undergoing change. Each member of the department wanted to be a larger piece of the whole body of research.

As I review this process, it is easy to see the good I found in learning teams. In each course I took, the learning teams continued to support each person in the course and constantly encouraged the members of the team to remain focused on the end goal: to attain their doctorate.

Unfortunately, not all learning teams operate successfully. I learned from personal experience that some team members do not always fulfill their duties, which can cause feelings of frustration, anger, dissatisfaction, and disenchantment. Fortunately, I experienced this feeling only once, and it highlighted how important it is to establish trust, elicit support from the other team members, and communicate openly, honestly, and respectfully.

No, teamwork is not always easy to manage. In fact, I once encountered the ugly aspect of a learning team when my assigned team had to perform an evaluation of each team member's performance on a final team project. The honest feedback provided on the evaluation created a rift that remained with one particular team member throughout the remaining series of courses. After that I did not feel as comfortable as I would have liked with that team member, but I did indeed learn from the experience. In life, we often have to find comfort in discomfort. We have to face challenge with a positive attitude and embrace each learning experience we face.

Learning teams are a vital part of the online learning process. Throughout my doctoral journey, I learned the true value of teams in a virtual environment and within an organization. My personal indicator of success was the attainment of my terminal degree and hearing about the same achievement from each of my respected cohort members. My organization received a seasoned team leader with the knowledge, skills, and abilities to work with and build teams that function effectively and efficiently.

Chapter 6: Residencies and Colloquia for Online Learners

Cheryl Szyarto

Depending on the learning institution, as discussed in chapter 1, distance learning doctoral programs may include residencies, or periods of time during which learners must engage in on-campus academic exercises and activities. Individuals may prefer distance learning doctoral programs without residency requirements if they are unable or prefer not to travel to their university's campus. Programs with limited residency requirements incorporate brief periods of study on campus, such as weekend workshops, weeklong seminars, or a combination of each. In some cases, online doctoral learners may be obliged to participate in more extensive residencies, where attending one or more classes on campus is required for degree completion.

Strategically selecting an online doctoral program is essential if prospective students want to invest their time and money wisely. In advance of selecting an online doctoral program, prospective students will not only want to research university accreditation, reputation, and tuition cost, among other factors, but they will also need to explore and understand the corresponding residency requirements of each online degree program. In advance of completing program applications, conducting an honest appraisal of personal and professional needs and preferences is essential if learners are going to succeed at selecting the most suitable online program for them.

Purpose of Residencies

The overarching goals and objectives, or overall purpose, of doctoral residencies will likely vary in scope and sequence from one learning institution and online degree program to the next. Likewise, some residencies may be credit bearing while others may not be. As previously noted, some online doctoral programs may have no residency requirements at all, while others may have residency components ranging from limited to extensive. Despite the probable variances in residency schedules, costs, and requirements, universities with online degree programs typically design associated on-campus residencies for the purpose of affording students the opportunity to engage with experienced, professional faculty and fellow cohort members in a hands-on, synchronous manner, thereby expanding and enriching the online learning experience.

When considering which online doctoral program to pursue, students will want to consider dissertation requirements, as well as if and how participating in the possible residency components will facilitate dissertation research and writing. Ideally, selecting a learning institution with a structured residency component will prove to be very valuable to doctoral learners who require coaching and mentoring beyond what can be offered asynchronously in the distance-learning classroom.

Advantages

Despite such variables as cost, frequency, and program-specific objectives, the advantages of doctoral residencies are relatively consistent from one university to the next. Even though individuals may allow personal biases and assumptions to influence their perceptions of each doctoral residency's value in light of the range of associated variables noted, residencies can provide learners with social, academic, and professional networking opportunities.

At my first doctoral residency, I forged a meaningful friendship with two fellow cohort members, who, throughout the remainder of our online doctoral studies, served as key figures in my academic and emotional support network. Our friendship has evolved over the years and, despite being separated by physical space and time, we have remained committed to holding annual three-day reunions in varied locales, during which time we reconnect, reminisce, and reflect upon our shared learning experiences, on how we have allowed such experiences to shape us personally and professionally, and about how we intend to maximize the return on our academic investments. Our friendship is priceless.

From an academic standpoint, each of the three doctoral residencies I attended was tremendously valuable. To understand the academic value each residency held and the impact it had on my performance as a student, let us compare, for a moment, a new doctoral learner writing a dissertation to a novice violinist rehearsing with a symphony. To facilitate the aforementioned comparison, allow the learner's doctoral cohort to symbolize the violinist's orchestra. After each orchestra rehearsal, the committed violinist, once leaning with fellow instrumentalists toward cacophony, is closer to achieving a desired state of harmony. Similarly, after each residency, the committed doctoral student, once flustered and overwhelmed alongside fellow cohort members, is closer to perfecting the collaborative teaming, research, critical thinking, and writing skills necessary to design, propose, and carry out a technically accurate and conceptually coherent dissertation study. Indeed, the one-on-one, face-to-face coaching and mentoring provided by qualified faculty at each consecutive residency led to a new stage of personal transformation, professional development, and academic growth in the dissertation writing process.

In addition to the social and academic advantages of each doctoral residency, learners cannot overlook the professional networking possibilities associated with the face-to-face meeting of individuals, who have a variety of professional connections to share and experiences from which to draw in the collaborative teaming process. At my second residency, for example, I was fortunate enough to meet a fellow cohort member, with whom I had not previously had the opportunity to work in the asynchronous online classroom. This particular individual, I later discovered, became a Program Director at a reputable West Coast university. Thanks to lines of communication opened at the second scheduled doctoral residency for our doctoral cohort, I learned of employment opportunities with the same university for which my fellow cohort member worked. While I relied on my academic and professional qualifications to secure my current teaching position with the same West Coast university, a professional recommendation and the knowledge of position openings came from my fellow cohort member. Indeed, doctoral residencies prompt valuable and unique professional networking opportunities.

Challenges

Among the varied considerations for learners in preparation for each residency, they cannot overlook the importance of proactively exploring potential residency scheduling conflicts and associated residency expenses not already incorporated into tuition costs. Learners must examine work responsibilities and family obligations prior to scheduling each residency with an academic program advisor. Researching related residency expenses (e.g., travel, lodging, and food) is essential if a student hopes to budget appropriately for such expenses.

While many challenges associated with doctoral residencies vary in nature from one individual to the next, I can share from my experiences the challenges I faced during each of my three scheduled residencies. Perhaps by sharing the residency-related challenges I faced as a doctoral learner, I will enable prospective doctoral students to be proactive in preparing for each of their residencies in order to avoid or cope with similar challenges.

Preparing for my first residency differed from preparing for my second and third residencies. Prior to my first residency, which was scheduled immediately after my first course in the doctoral program, I was filled primarily with excitement and enthusiasm. I was eager to embark upon the adventure that awaited me. I learned that from one residency to the next, my feelings before, during, and after the experience varied greatly. With each passing residency, I became further invested in the program; by my final residency, I was so emotionally, financially, and cognitively invested in the program that the activities, events, interactions, and outcomes of each carried much greater weight. Consequently, one challenge I faced was coping with the occasional setbacks I would experience from one residency to the next. But setbacks are temporary. I learned to view them as real life opportunities to apply the critical and creative thinking skills necessary to navigate through life.

Regarding setbacks or challenges—indeed, I experienced at least one during each residency. During my first residency, I learned first-hand the challenges associated with team formation. One goal of my first residency was to explore the collaborative learning model around which the university designed my doctoral program of study. Consequently, I learned on the spot how to manage the inherent challenges associated with team forming, norming, storming, and performing. My first residency learning team was comprised of a 60-something-year-old priest from the U.S.-Mexican border, a 30-something-year-old judge's daughter and single mother of two from Texas, and a former U.S. marine from southern

Virginia in his late twenties. While it was a challenge at my first residency to be teamed up with such a diverse group of individuals holding views that, in many cases, contrasted starkly with my own, I learned how to employ our differences to our collective advantage. Learning how to skillfully handle the challenges associated with team development in the face-to-face setting facilitated productivity in the online team setting thereafter.

During my second residency, when my emotional, financial, and cognitive investment was even greater, I made the startling discovery that the lead mentor of my dissertation committee was less than an ideal match for me. In the midst of my second residency, I faced the challenge of relieving my first doctoral mentor of her duties in spite of the year she and I had invested in our student-mentor relationship. While it might have been easier on many levels to grin and bear our differences and press on in spite of them, I listened to the advice of my cohort members who had gone through similar experiences and did what was in the best interest of my studies—I researched, interviewed, and hired a new doctoral mentor all before my second residency concluded. In retrospect, that was the single most important decision I had made in the course of my four-year doctoral journey. To this day, I remain indebted to the very brilliant, incredibly talented, and remarkably inspirational woman who, through my university years, I was fortunate enough to have serve as my lead mentor throughout the dissertation writing process.

Perhaps the greatest challenge I encountered was at residency 3, during which time my cohort members and I, among other responsibilities, had to present our dissertation proposals to one another in the presence of qualified faculty who were prepared to assess our progress to date. The peer pressure almost got the best of me. To my left sat Ike, a businessman and aspiring politician from Nigeria, whose dissertation proposal draft looked to be over 200 pages in length with a very lengthy list of research references. While I realize that quality of work is more important than quantity, my weak, incomplete proposal, reflecting one rather than the three required chapters, stood in stark contrast to Ike's. Then of course there was Ann to my right. Ann introduced herself as a Certified Public Accountant, who owned and operated her own accounting firm, and who *coincidentally* was light years ahead of our cohort in terms of dissertation progress. Ann was several months ahead of the university's suggested schedule for dissertation proposal submission.

Ike and Ann, while both inspiring and encouraging, sure did a number on my self-esteem because I allowed their progress to influence the perception of my own. I concluded my final residency acknowledging what I already knew: Everyone learns and performs according to his or her own pace and style.

My family obligations, work demands, and academic responsibilities grew exponentially from one residency to the next. In turn, I learned to accept that every step forward, however great or small, was a step in the right direction and was one step closer to program completion. No challenge would impede me from fulfilling my goal of successfully completing the doctoral program in which I was enrolled.

Related Tips

Preparing for each Residency

As previously noted, residency-bound doctoral learners will want to schedule their residencies proactively, if possible, so as not to pose related scheduling conflicts at work and home. Likewise, researching related residency expenses, outside of costs incorporated into tuition, is necessary for appropriate budgeting purposes. In addition, reviewing residency goals, objectives, and prerequisite readings and assignments is critical to arriving academically prepared to each residency. Identifying the name and contact information for your residency coordinator will prove helpful. Investigate dress code, if not already detailed and communicated by the residency coordinator, and request a residency itinerary from the residency coordinator if not provided in advance. Ensure reliable transportation to, from, and during residency if not scheduled for you by your academic advisor or residency coordinator. Consider the value of personal and professional networking at each residency, and carry along business or contact cards detailing your preferred contact information to facilitate networking opportunities.

Surviving and Maximizing each Residency

Surviving each residency is quite simple if you prepare appropriately and follow a few essential ground rules: Eat well-rounded, healthy meals, get adequate rest each evening, and devise an individualized plan for attaining the personal and professional goals associated with each required residency. Be willing to accept constructive criticism and determine how you will use such feedback to your advantage. Engage in critical thinking; set aside your biases and assumptions, maintain an open mind, and remain focused, objective, and analytical. Most important, engage in reflexive learning, and be more aware of your own learning. Enjoy each and every residency experience, and celebrate your accomplishments and personal discoveries along the way!

Chapter 7: Inspiration to Dissertation

Leilani Longa

There is a level of excitement, enthusiasm, and eagerness as well as anxiety, anguish, and apprehension around selecting a dissertation topic. Most doctoral students have a passion about what type of study would be of interest, while others feel indifferent or unsure of choosing a topic to study. These feelings of either comfort or concern are natural for students to experience. Going through these phases of emotion is common; however, once the process of thinking about ideas for a topic begins, one will find inspiration to be a driving force. The source of inspiration may come from a number of aspects of one's environment. It may spring from something that happened at work, a newspaper article you read, an encounter with a friend, or an event in a child's life. Whatever it may be, something has stimulated your mind and motivated you to move down a path and start to develop an initial idea of a dissertation topic to study.

Selecting a dissertation topic may take a little more time and energy than you think. To some, selecting a topic is simple, while for others it may be complex and quite complicated. There are informal guidelines to follow when deciding on a topic that each doctoral student should know. This chapter provides valuable information that will help develop and organize your thoughts and will assist you in keeping and staying focused. Also included in this chapter is an explanation of how to get started, dealing with such topics as inspiration and ideas, narrowing the focus of the topic of study so that it is attainable, managing and organizing the topic for relevant and germane information that is appropriate to the study, and understanding the difference between substantive research and original research.

Planting the Seed

What happens when a seed is planted in a garden? In order for the seed to grow into a healthy plant, it requires nutrients like sunlight, water, soil, and air. Once the seed is planted and cared for it may grow into a beautiful budding rose bush. Using this analogy and applying it to a doctoral dissertation topic, in order for the idea of a dissertation topic to grow, it needs to be developed, refined, and enhanced so that it can become a valued contribution to scholarly work. Once the idea for a topic is set in motion, it opens the door to infinite possibilities of areas to study. At one extreme, there may be a sense of chaos and panic in the student's mind, but at the other, there may be a sense of calmness and peace. After the seed has been planted, it is up to the student to decide on how best to approach the decision to select a dissertation topic.

As you settle into your program, whether that program is healthcare administration, education, information technology, or management, you will gain knowledge and begin to think about several topics that may be interesting to write about. At each point throughout the program, the instructors begin to encourage the students to think about a topic that motivates them and that they believe is significant. At this stage you may find yourself contemplating a plethora of ideas that may be of interest. Some ideas may be grandiose and others a bit simpler, depending on your level of ambition. During further interaction with instructors and other cohorts, the buzzing of ideas spreads, leaving you thinking about what to study, the one burning topic that will be the trajectory for your entire doctoral dissertation journey. It may not be easy, but there is a place to start, and that is the first step.

Getting Started

To begin the process of selecting a topic, it is easy to start by brainstorming ideas no matter how big or small. These ideas may be driven by work, society, home, government, education, media, or any number of other factors. Instructors will begin to ask you questions about what interests you, the type of career field you are in or would like to be in, current events happening around the world, life experiences that have affected you, the possibility of studying something completely new and undiscovered, or possibly studying something that has already been studied, but may need to be updated or revisited due to new or changing technology, processes, systems, laws, regulations, or behaviors and societal influences.

What is Your Inspiration/Passion?

As a student, you will begin to be motivated and inspired by many ideas. You will find instructors suggesting that you choose a topic that you are inspired or passionate about— something that sparks your interest and that you will not get bored learning, studying, or writing about for the next few years. Are you inspired by helping others through health and education, or does the invention and creation of new technology to keep others safe inspire you? What are you passionate about? Could it be for all children to have a successful education or the ability to help countries in need from natural disasters? Students find their inspiration and passion in various things, and it is important to find out what that is for you. A good place to start is writing out your ideas on a spreadsheet or flip chart or in a document, whichever is easiest for you. From your list of ideas, think about which ideas truly jump out at you, those that make a statement or that resonate within you, those that excite you. A natural next step is to begin crossing out those ideas that no longer interest you and keep the ones that you do like. This step begins the process of narrowing down your ideas for dissertation topics to study.

Where to Go and Where to Look for Ideas

Ideas are all around you. Look for them everywhere: at work, home, school, church, newspapers, in the community; look on the Internet, in peer-reviewed magazines and websites, libraries, media, television, print, and magazines for ideas on current events or new areas that may be worth studying. After you have focused in on and narrowed down your ideas, it's a good practice to begin a review of documents and articles to see if the ideas have been studied before or if, perchance, no previous studies or information exist. At this point, the research review does not need to be extensive. This level of review needs to be a broad overview of what has been or not been studied or researched. Some students find, as they go through this type of review, that other ideas are uncovered for potential dissertation topics. A few major topics start to become clearer and begin to stand out above the rest.

Whom to Ask

When in doubt, ask around to help stimulate inspiration and ideas. To assist in narrowing your scope, it is good to ask experts in your field of study or topic of interest. It is also helpful to ask experts at work, at school, and in the community; or corporate leaders, such as peers, instructors, coworkers, and bosses; and ask individuals in your corporate network, educational network, and social or community groups. Seeking guidance and input from others is a good first step, especially if you are unsure about what you would like to study, need additional insight, or would like to use others as a springboard to get started. For students who require more clarification for understanding, instructors and former doctoral students are excellent resources to field questions one may have about choosing a dissertation topic. If you think you already have a solid topic to study, be sure to review your topic with an instructor or peer.

Scope: Don't Try to Save the World

It is important to know and understand your scope of study. You should ask several questions before settling on a topic. Do you have the capacity? Do you have the time? Do you have the resources? This is the time to narrow your focus on a topic of study, taking into account many competing factors. Instructors will encourage you to select something a) that you can study and complete within one to two years, and b) that is accessible in your realm, and hence is within your grasp. In sum, the topic should be attainable and manageable. A topic such as studying the leadership styles of Chief Executive Officers (CEOs) from the top Fortune 500 companies may not be feasible due to possible time constraints, limitations of agreement from and accessibility to the CEOs, and scheduling conflicts that may arise, especially if the student decides to interview each CEO. To make a study such as this more achievable it would be wise for the student to narrow the scope, for example, to interviewing the top 15 highest paid healthcare CEOs in Southern California. The scope and topic is more narrowed and focused on a target population, location, and industry. The topic is reachable and the goal of completing the research is achievable within a reasonable time frame, which for most students is between one and two years, possibly three if necessary.

Small but Delicious Slice: Choosing a Solid, Rewarding, and Scholarly Topic

Once you have narrowed your topic and your scope to something attainable, take that small slice and make the most of it. Become the expert in your topic. Research and investigate everything possible. Learn as much as possible, and obtain as much real world experience as you can about the topic.

Whether you are doing a quantitative, qualitative, or mixed methods study, there is always something new to discover and explore or something more to elaborate upon. The topic that you choose should be something that you believe in and that will make a difference. Select something that others can use and that is a true contribution of your work to the program, organization, industry, or community. The scholarly topic should have value and should be rewarding to you and to others who will gain a deeper knowledge and understanding from the study. The scholarly topic should be one you're proud of and that you would be willing to present to others because it may become your legacy.

Honing In

It is time to hone in on the selected topic. Now that your topic has been narrowed, the next step is to sharpen it up and improve upon it. You should begin thinking about the geographic area, demographic information, methodology, industry, and population to be studied. These aspects may already have been addressed during your thought process in narrowing your topic, your initial document review, and asking others for insight and feedback. The picture of your study will suddenly become clearer and your direction more focused. Once the topic has been selected, refined, reviewed, and approved by the instructor, you will be ready to design and initiate a game plan to begin the dissertation study.

Your Game Plan

What is your game plan? Now that you have a dissertation topic to study, think about why you have decided to study this topic. Understand what you would like to accomplish through your topic of study. Instructors will ask you to develop the study's problem and purpose statements . Each of these statements is more complex than one may think, but they are guiding principles to follow. Students are often given an outline for the dissertation, as well as a description of what should be included. When creating your game plan, it is important to follow this outline. Use the outline to create your timeline; set deadlines and due dates to have various sections or chapters completed. Pace yourself; you will need time to research and investigate your topic and decide on your study methodology.

What if I Want to Study A Topic that has Already Been Studied?

Oftentimes, students select a topic that has already been studied. If you want to do that, you will need to identify the one thing that will make your study unique and that will distinguish it from the others. You will be required to demonstrate how your research will enhance a previous study or contribute to new learning. The study may have been conducted in the United States, but not in Asia, or the study may be out of date and hence may need to be refreshed with current data due to new information or technology. A comparison study may be necessary to see if there has been a change or improvement from then until now. Previous research can be the basis of the study, which provides in-depth detail and background for building a foundation for your study. If you choose a topic that has already been studied, you will be allowed to contact the original author of the study to gain additional input and information on the thought processes and approaches the author used to conduct the study, as well as any lessons learned or recommendations for further research.

Managing Your Topic

Organizing and managing your topic is important. Sometimes you will gather broad information that needs to be narrowed. It is important to research the information that will compliment what you are trying to study. Focus on others' research that is similar to yours, use peer-reviewed publications, and those elements that can be defended. Remember to stay focused on your topic and not let it get out of hand. Do not include everything that you find because it may be unnecessary and inappropriate to your study. Focus on the facts and information that is relevant and pertinent. Students may find that their topic stretches across several disciplines. If a student selects a topic about the use and acceptance of health information systems among newly graduated physicians, the research for such a topic will include healthcare, technology, education, and organizational behavior disciplines all in one study. It is helpful to develop a literature review matrix to organize and manage your research for the selected topic.

Substantive and Original: Two Critical Terms

As a student, you will learn about two critical terms while researching your doctoral dissertation topic. These terms are substantive research and original research. Understand now that not all research is the same and that not all research is scholarly, peer-reviewed research. Peer review is the process by which scholarly work is reviewed and scrutinized by a panel of experts to determine the quality and reliability of the work before publication. You may come across an article that appears to be reliable; however, no rigorous review or evaluation by experts has been conducted for the validity and accuracy of the content within the document. Doctoral students should be cautious and wary of articles that have not been peer reviewed whether the research is substantive or original.

What is Substantive Research?

Substantive is defined by Merriam-Webster online as having a solid base, being substantial; having a firm basis in reality and being therefore important, meaningful, or considerable, the essence or essential element of a thing, as in "substantive information"; having substance and prompting thought, applying to the essential. Substantive research is based on longer-term research using relatively established methods. In substantive research the student is expected to gather information with the purpose of proving or supporting the topic of study. Substantive research is based on existing documents and studies that provide a foundation for the study.

What is Original Research?

Merriam-Webster online defines *original research* as "research that is not exclusively based on a summary, review, or synthesis of earlier publications on the subject of research; the production of new knowledge, it does not use as its primary basis the synthesis or review of previous publications on the subject of research." Students must be aware that original research is new and that it has no reference or resource base other than what is provided within the study. Original research offers new knowledge in its discipline. Students who base their study on original research have the privilege of proving, disproving, confirming, refuting, comparing, contrasting, and building upon existing knowledge in order to develop new knowledge. Conducting original research studies is common for doctoral dissertations. The level and rigor of the student's work increases through working on original research.

Personal Experiences

A professor once told me, during my year 2 residency when I presented my topic, that I could not save the world. I am only one person, and the time I had allotted to my study did not permit me to do what I wanted to do. The topic I presented was to study universal healthcare for the United States. Not realizing that this topic was larger than life, too far reaching, and hence unattainable in one year, I was completely shot down during my presentation. The instructor continued to share with me his perspective on my topic and how impossible it would be to conduct a study of this magnitude given my constraints. He further suggested for me to go back and think about another topic that would be much more attainable, focused, and simpler for me to achieve. He also threw out studying the morbidity of babies born in Hawaii. He further suggested that I study something unique to Hawaii in healthcare so that my study would be confined to reachable information and areas in my span of control.

I was quite disappointed and rather embarrassed by all of these developments; I was in a panic because I had only three days to figure out a good topic. That evening, I went to the student workroom and researched various topics that have been studied as well as other areas that needed further study. What came to mind was a new idea I had encountered at work: the use of electronic medical records. I did some research and found that there was limited information on electronic medical records and on top of that, no research on that topic had been done in Hawaii. I felt that this was a perfect topic to study, that I was not attempting to save the world, that it was in my realm and span of control, and that it was definitely attainable, given my parameters. The last day of residency, I presented my topic, and the instructor was pleased by it.

Afterward, he asked me if I wanted to have dinner with him and his daughter. I had not expected such an invitation because during the dreadful three days of residency, I felt as though he was picking on me and using me as an example in front of the class of what not to do—as if I had been born yesterday and had no clue. It was quite a blow to my ego and my self-esteem. I politely turned down his offer, but the one thing that brightened my spirit again was that he apologized to me for making me feel bad in class and told me that it was not his intention to do so at all. I felt so much better because by the last day of class, I was thinking that I had no hope, and I felt quite helpless. I was questioning about whether or not I could do this, but, although my spirit was broken for a moment, I regained my composure and the strength to move on in order to tackle and achieve my goal.

This brings me to the topic of this chapter: finding the inspiration for your dissertation. You will experience several refinements to your dissertation topic, but do not fear. This process is for the best, and it will be completely helpful in the end. If I had truly stuck with my original study of universal healthcare for America, I probably would not have been able to achieve my goal in a timely manner and might still be in school and not have graduated yet! Coincidentally, about two years later, on Sunday, March 21, 2010, our history-making first African-American President, Barack Obama, and Congress voted on and passed the Healthcare Reform Bill to provide every American with healthcare coverage.

I guess my original topic to save the world and provide universal healthcare was not only timely and something that was important to me, but was also important to the rest of the country as well. I am proud of where I started and where I ended in conducting my study and writing my dissertation. My next step is to contribute to society, to the healthcare industry, and to education in other ways; and maybe one day I will save the world—one small step at a time.

Chapter 8: Choosing a Mentor and a Committee

Melanie Magruder

I have actually engaged a mentor for various reasons throughout my lifetime. I was never told that I needed one; I just thought it was a good idea to follow the guidance of someone who knew how to accomplish goals that I had set. There are various definitions of a mentor, but the one I particularly like is someone who helps another to succeed in reaching positive goals.

It was during the second-year residency as a doctoral learner that I was told I needed a mentor to work with me during the dissertation writing and approval processes. We were given a few snippets prior to that time, but never any elaborative info to confirm exactly what that meant or how to approach such an order. Some of the learners knew a bit more than others, while several had no clue what to do. To help us gain an understanding, the school's administration had designed a process by which learners could find a mentor. Doctoral students are required to choose a mentor for the dissertation process. Actually, an entire committee is needed.

First, you might want to know exactly what a mentor is in this instance and why you as a doctoral student would need one. Think of it this way: you have started a new position at a company and have been deemed qualified for the position, but you do not have a clear understanding as to how you are going to accomplish the goals set forth in the role you have accepted. This is how the mentor helps: you do all of the work, and the mentor lets you know if it is going to be approved by those who will review your work. Others are involved who will help as well; they are your committee members. The mentor is part of the committee; however, he or she normally has the final approval and can override what the other members of the team have directed you to do.

The mentor and committee members are basically doctors who know how to guide the learner through the process of becoming a doctor. They understand the entire process, from selecting a topic to getting approval from the Dean. At times I thought they were totally against me, when in fact, they wanted me to be very successful. Why did I think they were against me, you may ask? The processes of choosing a topic, changing the methodology, and writing the chapters, *ad infinitum* are all clearly understood by the mentor and committee members, and not entirely by the learner. The lack of understanding can bring students to the point where they do not think that everyone is on the same team, but you will have to trust that these people have your success in mind and are aiming toward the same goal you are. . .earning your doctoral degree.

Sometimes you may need approval to move forward from a committee member or your mentor, and, to your surprise and dismay, you find that they are all inaccessible. What do you do? Well, you just have to wait because mentors are instrumental figures in your path toward dissertation completion, and you really cannot go around them. The solution here is to keep in contact with your mentor and committee members to find out if they have any planned time away. This will help create a schedule around what you need from them.

What if your mentor agrees to be on your team, but then tells you after your proposal is half-written that he or she cannot be on your committee anymore? The other members are not willing to take on that lead role because their plates are already full. Before selecting your mentor, you should ask your mentor certain questions, which might include the following: Have you done this before? What is your area of expertise? With which research methodologies are you most experienced? Why do you think we would be a good match? What is your availability? How do I reach you? How will we communicate? The learner should also have a good second or third person in line to interview as a mentor in the event the first choice does not work out as planned.

The selection process is up to you, within the school's guidelines. I found that it was best to have a mentor who was involved in the same area of profession and who had experience in mentoring other students through more than one methodology. Initially, I chose a mixed-methods project, but later changed to the qualitative method; my mentor had experience in both areas.

The committee members I chose also had experience in mixed, qualitative, and quantitative methods. The other key factor was that they knew each other and had been successful in assisting students with the dissertation process. There may be issues that you cannot afford to encounter if you don't know whether the mentor and committee members can work well together.

Chapter 9: Writing the Proposal— Chapters 1, 2, and 3

Andy Elliott and Melanie Magruder

A Conversation With Two Former Doctoral Students

Dr. M: Oh, how I wanted to save the world! I entered the program having many problems to solve. After several discussions with my cohort members, we decided that focusing on one specific need would suffice. From that understanding, there had to be one problem I could address (what a tall order, only one?!) Establishing a methodology was a little difficult at first because I really did not understand what I wanted to accomplish. Upon writing the prospectus, I considered mixed and quantitative methods. However, after researching those methods and narrowing down a goal, I decided that the qualitative method was the best way to address the problem. The qualitative method provides an opportunity to interview people and share their views with the world without crunching a lot of numbers. I wanted to produce a meaningful study by hearing and sharing the viewpoints of others.

Dr. A: I agree! I think understanding that I needed to start with a problem, develop a purpose, and select a methodology was a huge part of the process. I came into the program with a problem in my head. The problem is something in your proposal that should jump off the page. The reader needs to be able to clearly identify or recognize the problem statement. The problem statement should answer the question, "Why am I conducting this research anyway?"

You are then ready to establish the purpose for the research study. The purpose should be clearly stated with a simple sentence that begins with, "The purpose of the proposed study is...." Identifying the specific methodology makes the purpose even stronger. "The purpose of the proposed quantitative study is...." To help me understand the purpose, I created the following acronym:

P - Population identified

U - Understand method: qualitative, quantitative, or mixed

R - Research design coincides with research method

P - Proposed study includes appropriate methodology

O - Overt research design (it is clearly stated)

S - Selected variables are identified (when applicable)

E - Each geographical location is identified

The purpose for me was difficult because I couldn't decide upon a particular methodology. Were you able to decide your methodology quickly or was there a process you went through?

Dr. M: Boy, was there ever a process! It took a while to really understand the outcomes that I wanted and how I needed to get there. I discussed different methodologies with my mentor, doctoral graduates, fellow cohort members, and instructors. I had to research each of the three methodologies to determine which one would produce the paper I wanted to share with the world. My first choice was a mixed method; however, after careful research I concluded it was not necessary to have both quantitative and qualitative studies combined, as the goal I wanted to accomplish could be achieved through the qualitative method. My research lasted for approximately six months before I chose the methodology. I read papers and purchased books on the methodologies written by industry leaders in research. The bottom line is that my mentor had to approve the method, and I had to make my case about why I thought this was the best approach for my topic. It was long and tedious, but in the end, the process was worth every minute.

Dr. A: I must have bought a lot of the same books! I also think having strong colleagues helped guide me, but the push was always toward quantitative research, and that scared me to an extent. I have always been good at math, but I have never been a numbers person. I am all about reading, writing, and speaking; numbers spoke a language that I didn't always understand. Then I met someone that began to speak about qualitative research and how it dealt with patterns, perceptions, and meaning found when interpreting the spoken or written word. That was my light bulb moment! I created another acronym:

Q - Qualifies

U - Universal

A - Attitudes by

L - Listening to

I - Individual

T - Thoughts

A - And

T - Translating

I - Important

V - Vital

E - Experiences

I was then introduced to Creswell, whose book on qualitative inquiry and research design gave some solid protocols and designs that I could use. Even then I was unaware that there were many types of qualitative studies. I began to look at each and questioned professors while completing my other course work. The five qualitative studies available to me were a narrative-biographical study, a phenomenological study, a grounded theory study, an ethnographic study, and a case study. Now came the difficult task of choosing the one that works for me. Did you use Creswell as well?

Dr. M: Yes, I read several of Creswell's books on research methods and became very enlightened and confused at the same time. I wanted to do it all. Nevertheless, the material I read of Creswell's and other authors on the topic of research helped me narrow down my decision to use a qualitative method for my dissertation. Although it took awhile to research this conclusion, the knowledge I gained is priceless, as I can share my experience with others with the hope of helping them make an informed decision.

Dr. A: Very well said! I think it is important to mention as well that the purpose of a dissertation is not to change the world. Time is an element that must be considered. I thought I would have time to do a mixed-method study, which would have taken me nearly two years to get the research and analyze my findings, so I set out to do a study that was relevant and manageable, and that would adequately cover my chosen topic. Then, once my dissertation was complete I would have reached the necessary plateau to further study my chosen topic and take as much time as possible. Sometimes we just need to get it done now and save the world later!

Dr. M: [Chapter 2,] the literature review, seemed to be very exhaustive in the beginning. However, once I started the process, it proved to be very beneficial in the long run. Having compiled a literature list really helped me in preparing a paper that was approved. One thing I learned during this process was that I did not keep a good record of my references that were cited. It is a good practice to keep a separate document, outside of the actual paper, that lists all of the references cited in the paper. If this is not done, the learner will run the risk of losing the cited references.

Dr. A: I agree that the literature review will be better if the information is organized in a clear manner. I created a chart in Excel and separated my literature into categories such as historical significance, definitions and terms, current findings, and relevance to leadership. I am confident that there are many different ways to organize the information, but having a visual aid and keeping track of the number and relevance of each topic will assist in research development and tracking of the articles. Peer-reviewed articles are essential to the authenticity of your study. Most online libraries have a way for graduate and doctoral students to search for peer-reviewed articles only. This is an excellent tool and a great place to start the research on your selected topic.

Dr. M: Great points, Dr. A. The peer-reviewed material is located in most online libraries, which makes the online learning process that much more convenient for the learner. I found a plethora of material online that supported my literature review for the research I conducted. Organization is very important as some of the authors may produce much of the material that is collected. It is important to confirm that the literature review represents the research you are conducting, as this is a major section in the proposal.

Chapter 10: The Academic Review Board

Sybil DeVeaux

Yes, There Really are Review Boards

Once you have written Chapters 1, 2 and 3, you may believe you have earned the right to relax. Universities require all doctoral students to undergo a rigorous assessment to earn research approval from a panel of experts, known as the Review Board (RB). Most universities have what is known as the Academic Review Board, which is a panel of qualified individuals who review the components of a student's dissertation proposal to ensure that each component meets university requirements. The remainder of this chapter contains a description of each component of the dissertation proposal (Chapters 1-3), which the RB will assess. The following information expands upon the contents of previous chapter 9 of this text ("Writing the Proposal - Chapters 1, 2, and 3").

Purpose

All proposals must follow detailed guidelines; therefore, when the proposal is written, but before you submit it to the RB, you need to ensure that everything you have written meets the requirements. You may be wondering: what really is the Review Board? The first review is a blind review for your proposal. What this means is that there should be no identifying information within your document; therefore, your name should not appear, and neither should the names of your committee members.

Procedure

The first year of the doctoral journey involves the successful completion of required courses through which the student displays his contribution to the field of study and expertise. By the end of year 1, the proposal should be written and the student ready to undergo the review by a mentor and committee members. Writing the proposal is a tedious task involving many components that are required to be scrutinized by various reviews.

Review Board

Yes, this is when you begin to bite your nails, waiting for and wondering about a response from the Review Board (RB). The RB is good at responding in a timely manner, so do not panic; and the better prepared you are, the easier the process will be. One good way to safeguard against repeated submissions to the RB is to use of a self-assessment checklist. Your school may provide one for you; if not, it would be a good idea to create one. This checklist is a very important document for all learners. When the RB is through with the review, your document will be returned along with the results. Avoid using unnecessary words and stay within the checklist guidelines.

Sample Writing

The following guide may be of help prior to RB submission.

The Introductory Paragraph

The introductory paragraph sets the tone of the proposal and ultimately the dissertation. Ensure that a) this paragraph does not have a heading; b) the dissertation topic is introduced; and c) the discussion reflects an overview of chapter 1. This section may be approximately one-half to three-quarters page long (note that the length of the sections will vary considerably according to the differing requirements of various universities. Lengths given here are average and are suggestions only).

Background

What is the inspiration for your dissertation? Is your problem based on personal experience? Whatever your inspiration, be sure it "is of important social concern or theoretical interest," according to the checklist from one online university. The discussion needs to specify why the problem is important and if the research will help society. This section may be approximately two and a half pages long.

Statement of the Problem

Four parts are required in this section:

1. General problem
2. Specific problem
3. Introductory words
4. General population

The *general problem* is the observation that identifies the need for the study; for example, the general problem may be that many factors influence leadership styles.

The *specific problem* is that proposed for the research; the problem statement is clear, concise, and reflective of the purpose statement. This section is straightforward, with all that is needed being identification of the specific problem; for example, the specific problem for a qualitative case study may be that many organizational leaders are skeptical about the leadership styles of newly graduated doctors. Effective leaders are authentic, self-aware, transparent, and unafraid of challenges.

Specific words, referred to as *introductory words*, are necessary to describe the method and design of the study. Here is an example of an appropriate introduction to this section:

The qualitative case study will explore and identify the patterns and types of leadership styles of recent doctoral graduates from the university level to determine the influence of their learning on their immediate working environment.

To identify the *general population*, use words that are specific to the problem:

The qualitative case study will explore the relationships among leadership styles of 40 recent doctoral graduates at the university level, who work in the eastern United States. The study will also explore the effects of communication, diversity, and organizational culture on the leadership styles.

Purpose

This section that deals with the research purpose has seven parts, each of which may be about three-quarters of a page:

Research method. What research method do you plan to use? Selection is based on (a) qualitative; (b) quantitative; and (c) mixed. Be strategic in your selection, that is, if you are proficient at writing, you may want to choose a qualitative method. Again, if you like statistics, use the quantitative method.. The mixed method approach, of course , will include both qualitative and quantitative methods. Once the research method is identified, clearly state the research design and ensure that the design is appropriate. If you select a quantitative approach, you will need to determine and identify your research variables: independent, dependent, relationships and comparisons. Next, identify the specific population and geographic location.

Significance of the study. The significance of the study is divided into two parts and may be about a page. Why did you decide to do the study and why is it important? How does your study contribute to other studies and more important, how does it contribute to the field of leadership? Once you are able to answer those questions you will be on the right track.

Nature of the study. At this point you should have enough confidence to write an overview of the appropriateness of your research method. Why did you select the method? Are you able to accomplish your goals with the selected method or would another method be more appropriate? Always remember to reiterate the purpose of the study. In this section, you will also need to address the literature search, that is, the various topics on which your study is based. Here is an example:

> Searches for the literature review included peer-reviewed journals, recent doctoral dissertations,

scholarly books, academic books, and business books that focused on immigrants in government agencies, leadership, advancement barriers, and cultural development. Title searches for the qualitative case study included (a) communication (b) diversity and (c) organizational culture.

The section may be between 1 and 5 pages long, so you have an opportunity to impress your readers about the importance of the study. For example, your problem might be as follows: *An ethical dilemma exists among newly graduated doctors from the university and their immediate professional environment.* The reader will want to find out more about the problem. Think of this section as an oral presentation in which you must convince your audience that the study will benefit not only you, but also society and that it will affect future research on the topic. Do not be afraid to edit this section several times. The review board readers are very sensitive to how the sentences are phrased and will return your document with a low rating if it does not meet the standards.

At this stage you may wish to find other supporting documents just to add credence to your work. This is when you ask yourself: How much do I want this degree? Will I be able to convince others of the urgency of this problem? Most important, will I accomplish my goal and thus bring change?

Hypotheses or research questions. Be specific and base your hypotheses or questions on the purpose of your study. What is the relationship or comparison of the questions about the research focus? Be descriptive in your narrative and include your research questions if your method is qualitative. On the other hand, in addition to the research questions, if you are using a quantitative method, you may need to include proposed hypotheses and rationale for the hypotheses. Talk to your audience; remember you are on the podium and will need to discuss your work. This section has a length of 1 to 5 pages.

Conceptual or theoretical framework. How does your study fit in with similar studies? You need to describe the important issues and perspectives, and highlight any controversies that you encounter. This section should be two to four pages in length, and the checklist may recommend four parts, namely:

1. An overview of the broad theoretical area of the research

2. An overview of the proposal's fit within the area of research

3. Important issues, perspectives and controversies in the field and

4.   Reflection of knowledge and familiarity with the historical, germinal current literature in the research area.

Definitions. While writing your proposal, you will use certain terminologies and the reader will find it helpful if some of the terms are defined. This section may be about one page in length. You *must* cite every definition. Here is an example:

The following definitions are presented to give the reader a common understanding of key terms used in the qualitative case study. The section includes terms that are specific to leadership, communication, diversity and organizational culture. The following terms are defined and where necessary, definitions are supported with citations.

Executive Orders. Executive orders are legally binding orders used in the operation of government agencies by officials in their observation of established policies (Fox, 1999). Civil service leaders are expected to abide by the letter of executive orders.

One-in-three rule. The one-in-three rule is a provision of civil service law and City personnel rules, that allows agencies to pass over the top test-takers on a civil service list in favor of another, lower-scoring candidate from among the top three. The one-in-three system allows rampant abuse and presents opportunities for favoritism, discrimination, and patronage (Allen, 2008; Roberts, 2007).

Assumptions. The section that deals with assumptions is between one quarter and half a page in length. Be sure to identify any assumptions, give a rationale, and use different perspectives. The following example may be of help to you:

In the qualitative case study, a number of assumptions applied. The first assumption was that the experiences of the participants would be comparable to other immigrants in similar situations. The second assumption was that the selected demographics would become a benchmark for the way other immigrants are advanced. The third assumption was that participants would be honest and not attempt to bias the data when relating their experiences. The fourth assumption was that degreed immigrants in leadership positions as well as those who were prepared for leadership in terms of education and experience but were not yet leaders would candidly share their experiences. The rationale was that participants who candidly shared their experiences would not mislead the interviewer.

Scope, limitations, and delimitations. This section is about 1-2 pages in length and discusses the topic. Within this section the number of participants, data collection method, and aim of the study are described. What limitations do you anticipate? Limitations may be due to the number of people who agree to voluntarily participate in the study, sample size, participants not being candid, or the applicability of the research to other situations. See the following example:

A sole researcher, who is also an English-speaking immigrant, conducted the qualitative case study; thus researcher influence may have led to a biased perspective. Researcher bias could have also influenced interpretation of the interviews and observations. Other limitations included (a) ethical concerns wherein participants might face retaliation from their supervisors; (b) participants' emotions, which could have created a problem because of the sensitive nature of their answers; and (c) use of the NVivo8 software, which, because respondents may not have answered truthfully, could have resulted in erroneous assumptions or false interpretations.

Delimitations are threats to the external validity and generalization of the results of the study to the greater population. Here is a sample:

The nature of a case study was the in-depth focus on a small number of cases; however, the small sample of cases may have limited transferability of the findings, thus creating delimitations in the study. Transferability of the results of the study to other underrepresented groups outside the civil service may not be possible.

Summary. Do not write too much in your summary–a half to one page is enough. One university checklist advises:

1. Discussion *summarizes key points* presented in chapter
2. Supporting citations are given for key points.
3. Chapter summary ends with transition discussion/sentence to next chapter
4. Information is presented in a discussion context, rather than simply stated or listed.

Continue to use the checklist to write chapters 2 and 3.

On average, chapter 2 may be 20-30 pages long, and chapter 3 may be 10-25 pages in length. When in doubt, download other dissertations from the library.

Academic Review Results

Your grade determines your future--that is, you will either need to make changes or will be given the green light to proceed with writing your dissertation. You should aim for the highest ratings, and certain precautions will help you. Did you hire an editor? A dissertation editor is highly recommended because if you are like most of us, you will be tired of reading and rereading, and you may not recognize errors. When you are comfortable with your proposal, send a copy to your mentor and to each committee member. Set yourself deadlines, and try to adhere to them. There will be times when your committee members are tardy, and you may find it necessary to remind them that you are on a tight schedule. Once your mentor approves the proposal, submit a copy to the Human Services Review Board. In the meantime, do not expect an approval for your first submission. Some students submit multiple times prior to gaining approval.

Personal Experiences

When I first wrote my proposal, I had no idea of what was expected because even though I had a dissertation template, understanding how to use it properly was a challenge. Additionally, I had a mentor who was experiencing the process for the first time, so we both struggled. My main source of support was my cohort. We discussed problems and shared information. Another source of support came from students I met during residencies. Every piece of information received was shared with our friends.

Deadlines are extremely important if you plan to graduate; however, not everyone observes deadlines. You are responsible for meeting the deadlines and must ensure you manage your timeline effectively, even if you have to send reminders your mentor and committee members. I remember e-mailing my committee members to remind them of important deadlines; if and when that did not work, I got on the telephone and checked to see how much longer each member would need to fulfill the task at hand. Editors, if extremely busy, may overlook deadlines. Remember, you are the boss of your proposal; members of your team are on the team to help you. If this is not the case, then take the necessary action to make this process a success; be honest and remember your goals. Keep in mind that you are to be respectful in whatever action you take.

Chapter 11: The Human Research Protection Review Board

Sybil DeVeaux

The Human Research Protection Review Board, referred to as the Institutional Review Board (IRB) at some universities, is designed to review the proposal package to determine that all of the requirements from the Office for Human Research Protection are met. Two independent reviewers, who are responsible for protecting the subjects, staff this RB. The reviewers also review the proposal and consent forms for completeness, accuracy, and quality. Year 3 is very important for each doctoral student because it marks the end of the beginning, and the beginning of the end. Once chapters 4 and 5 are written, which will be discussed later in this text, it is time for a big sigh of relief—you are nearly there. At this point, it becomes extremely important that the following requirements are addressed for purposes of the RB application: (a) human subjects research; (b) general purpose of study; (c) subject selection; (d) benefits of study; and (e) confidentiality.

Human Subjects Research

If human subjects are used in a research study, special care is needed to ensure their proper treatment. Researchers must ensure that no harm will come to the subjects. You will have to complete a designated questionnaire for approval.

General Purpose of the Study

Why is your study necessary and how does it serve the other disciplines? Examine other literature to glean what this means. The general purpose of qualitative research methods is to examine human behavior in the social, cultural, and political contexts in which it occurs. The qualitative method is carried out through a variety of tools, such as interviews, historical methods, case studies, and ethnography, usually resulting in qualitative primary data. Qualitative research is a type of educational research that allows the researcher to collect data consisting mainly of words that are analyzed for themes.

The quantitative study, to the contrary, predicts outcomes; contains specific, narrow questions; involves numerical data collection; and requires the use of mathematical procedures to analyze the numbers. The quantitative method also focuses on variables, uses many cases, and does not reflect the emotional attachment of the researcher.

In some instances neither the qualitative nor quantitative methodology will satisfy the requirements of a study, so researchers use both approaches. Such a blend is known as the mixed methodology. While the mixed method offers a more concise picture of the study and produces a conclusion, it also calls for extensive data collection in both qualitative and quantitative forms.

Subject Selection

Subject selection is an important component of every study and many approaches are available. The type of research you plan to conduct will dictate, in most cases, the minimum sample size needed for study completion. As with any study, the larger the sample is, the greater the study's external validity will be. Therefore, do not limit yourself to a very small sample size if at all possible. Remember, though, that researchers seldom examine everyone or everything in a population because what is important is relevance.

Benefits of the Study

The visionary leader creates a successful leader-follower relationship that benefits everyone. As a doctoral student, or visionary leader, why do you intend to conduct the study, and what will be the benefits of conducting it? Will your work create change? If you answer those questions in a positive manner, then your study is worth pursuing.

Confidentiality

Confidentiality is very important in order to protect the subjects. As such, you are required to include a statement of confidentiality. For my study I used the following:

Coworkers and acquaintances in civil service agencies will supply participants' contact information. Participants will be contacted through personal electronic mail, telephone, and face-to-face communication methods, and asked to sign an informed consent form prior to data collection (Appendix A). Prior to the study the participants will be promised that their personal information will remain confidential. In an effort to maintain confidentiality, data collected from participants (such as the signed informed consent form, demographic information, and participants' identities) will be kept in a locked safe at a secured location to which only the researcher has access.

In the qualitative case study, and to ensure confidentiality and anonymity, an identifier will be created and assigned to each participant. The identifier will be used during data collection and analysis, including "a two-digit number representing the order in which the participant was interviewed, the participant's level within the organization, and the date of the interview. Thus, for example, an identifier of 01EM01042009 means that an executive manager was the first person interviewed on January 4, 2009. The participant identifiers will be assigned a code name, such as Leader 1 (Appendix B).

The transcripts and audiotapes from the interviews will be kept in a locked desk, away from the identifiers. The participants' consent forms and electronic and paper data will be kept secure for a period of three years, at which time they will be destroyed.

The review board is very specific, so whatever you do, try to remain positive. If you become discouraged, reread this companion book and regain your confidence.

Personal Experiences

I remember the day that the representative from my university sent me an email to say that the Review Boards (RBs) had approved my work and that I should respond indicating receipt. The feeling is difficult to convey, but you will experience the same and life will have changed permanently....

Good luck, and I wish you all the joys that completing your dissertation will offer.

Chapter 12: Dissertation Conclusion and Recommendations

Leilani Longa

The final chapters of a dissertation include the data analysis, the conclusions of the study, and recommendations for further research. All of the elements in the previous chapters are presented in a summary or overview form. An in-depth discussion of the findings and data analysis take place in this chapter, as well as any implications, limitations, or suggestions for future research. In these chapters the student is expected to share what was learned and discovered throughout the study.

Data Analysis

Data analysis consists of the process of highlighting, breaking down, and organizing information into a format that is useful and meaningful. This step comes after the student has collected the data from the study. For some students, the data analysis process can be the most time consuming. Students are expected to score and code their data as appropriate, ensuring that the accuracy, validity, and reliability of the data are upheld along the way. Referring back to the research questions or to the hypothesis of the study is helpful in analyzing the data. Doing so keeps the student grounded in the foundation of the dissertation study. Sometimes, to the student's surprise, the results of the data analysis can turn out to be different from what was initially expected or predicted. The qualitative and quantitative research methods require differing approaches to conducting the data analysis.

Qualitative Analysis

When a student decides on a qualitative method of research, the analysis is qualitative as well. Qualitative analysis takes the narrative of the data collected as shared in the previous chapter of the dissertation and organizes this information to draw upon results. Qualitative analysis can be tricky at times because the student is expected to interpret the words or language of the study participants. Certain software applications can assist the student in analyzing the collected narrative data and categorize or group the data into common themes. Qualitative analysis does differ from quantitative analysis.

Quantitative Analysis

In a quantitative research method approach, the data analysis is sometimes heavily analyzed using statistical analysis. Usually, the data collected using quantitative methods are interpreted in numerical form rather than in narrative form, as alluded to earlier regarding qualitative research. As with qualitative analysis, software applications are available for analyzing quantitative data, using statistics that help to identify the relationships of the variables in the study. Some students may choose to hire an outside consultant to perform the data analysis, especially if they find it a bit challenging to analyze the data collected from their quantitative study.

Discussing Analysis and Findings

Chapter 5 of a dissertation provides a summary and discussion of the data analysis from the findings presented in Chapter 4. In this chapter, the student should discuss any major themes, sub-themes, results, and outcomes discovered during the analysis of the study. This is where a story is told; the information is no longer just data, and there is more substance. You begin to explain what happened during the study. The major themes, patterns, and findings that are prominent are elaborated upon, and this is where the student shows expertise and knowledge in his field of study.

When you are analyzing the data from your quantitative research, it is important to address the research question or hypothesis. During this process, the data should be scored and coded as appropriate. As a student, you will learn and understand the importance of assigning values to the data. This makes a significant difference during data analysis, and each finding is summarized in one or two sentences. When presenting the results, the student should discuss the central results, provide specific details, and explain why the results occurred as they did. During the discussion of the results, the student can provide information on any limitations identified that may have affected the results. This could be anything from missing data to an unexpected encounter or condition that transpired while the study was being conducted.

Qualitative research discussions of the data analysis and findings reflect on personal views of the study data. The student addresses the research question during the discussion, which is an overview of the major findings. The qualitative data are analyzed and coded into common themes or patterns similar to quantitative research. Interpretations and reports from the findings of the data should be presented in narrative summary form. The interpretation of the qualitative data is the section in which the student discerns the meaningfulness of the findings.

As with quantitative research, the student should also disclose any limitations of the study.

The analysis and findings of the data are discussed so that the information gathered makes sense and so that there is a level of understanding from the results of the study. The student is providing and interpreting fact from the findings. The results could either reveal answers that address the research question or support or dispute the research hypothesis. This discussion is essential in chapter 5 as it offers a complete picture of the study from beginning to end.

Implications for Leadership

Conducting a study for a dissertation has various implications for leadership. The outcomes of the study may be either positive or negative. The contribution to research in most cases produces a result, outcome, or answer to the students' research question or hypothesis. It is recommended that organizational leaders pay attention to and take notice of the implications from research findings. The implications could have significant consequences and repercussions or could result in valuable benefits and advantages for the organization and the leader. Acknowledging and addressing the outcome is an important first step.

Organizational leaders have the ability to influence and encourage others to take action. Organizational leaders can remove barriers and create opportunities for the organization to move forward. The leadership implications from findings within a research study could enhance, improve, or help the organization have a positive effect. In contrast, findings could worsen, hinder, or hurt the organization and result in negative leadership implications. Leaders set the tone of an organization and its culture; they are the visionaries whose support is necessary to drive change and improvements. The leader has the ability to develop a collaborative learning environment to move the organization toward success.

Recommendations

The recommendation section of Chapter 5 allows students to offer suggestions for scholarly research or proposals to organizational leaders. Now that the student has become an expert in his field, he is better able to provide guidance, advice, or counsel to others. The student has a knowledge and understanding of the big picture, and he sees things he did not see before conducting his doctoral research study. The student's recommendations may range from current process improvements to innovative technology. Additionally, the student may discover gaps in research or the need for continued research related to his study that may result in a recommendation for future research.

For Leaders

Recommendations for organizational leaders are significant in a study. During your research if you identify areas that could be useful to leadership, you are encouraged to make a recommendation for change, improvement, or further assessment. The student's scholarly research builds a substantial contribution to the area of study. Developing a proposal for the organization's leaders demonstrates that the student understands the study and its impact on the organization, industry, community, government, or the specific study group. Leadership recommendations associate areas of the findings with their effects on the organization or study.

The student is expected to provide a sound, logical, and factual analysis of the findings and to present a well-developed proposal or recommendation to the leader. The recommendation should resonate and make a connection with the leader, enabling him to recognize the importance of your proposal and provide meaning to the organization. The student's recommendation should provide information with which the leader may take action and make a difference for the organization.

For Future Research

In chapter 5, the recommendations for future research, the student provides information that identifies and acknowledges the need to explore specific and perhaps new areas of study. While conducting your study, you will sometimes find that a gap exists in the research. The gap provides an opportunity for future research. In the recommendation section, the student offers potential suggestions for future research. Recommended topics can stem from specific areas not covered in your study; areas discovered in your study, but which could use further focus and research; or potential areas that you may have discovered in your research that were never addressed or touched upon.

Future research could be based on the results gathered in your research. The outcome of the findings could drive the next steps in your research study. Sometimes a student begins his study by going in one direction, but later changes direction, which may lead to an entirely different conclusion or discovery. The suggestions the student makes for future research, which were concluded during the study, provide valuable next steps.

Personal Experiences

Writing the final chapter of the dissertation was, in my view, the easiest part. I had completed the hard work in the previous chapters of my research, conducted the study, and analyzed the findings. From that work, I truly felt like an expert in my field of study. I knew and understood my topic so well that I developed a calm confidence in the belief that I could write chapter 5 and be positive about it. The art of writing chapter 5, however, lies in not rewriting the previous chapters but in reviewing and highlighting the main points of the overall dissertation.

The study environment offers an entirely different perspective to students who have an opportunity to immerse themselves. I was fortunate to do just that in my study. I felt quite lucky to have the privilege of observing the study participants in their everyday surroundings. Being able to walk alongside the study participants and to live their life experiences was invaluable to me as a student and scholarly doctoral researcher. A student does not often encounter such a great benefit as this. I believe this experience worked to my advantage, and although it took much of my and the participants' time, I would not change a thing. This is what made writing chapter 5 less challenging and more inviting because I not only learned about the study, but also I lived it several times with the study participants. Actively participating in someone's life makes it easier to understand the study participants' lived experiences.

I had the privilege of presenting my findings and recommendations to the study participants and to the organizational leaders where I studied. My findings revealed new insights, which leadership and the study participants had not realized. The data also confirmed and validated several leadership issues. In my recommendation to the organizational leaders, I suggested that they conduct an assessment, identify gaps, develop training curriculum, address negative issues, conduct a cost benefit analysis, and create a strategic plan to address my findings and recommendations. The organizational leaders not only took my recommendations into consideration, but they also took action on several areas of my recommended proposal.

In the conclusion of my dissertation, I discovered the need for leadership's active involvement in an organization. Leading from an ivory tower does not always work, especially in the study I chose. The organization was entering a change in culture and technology. Such extreme change in management required extra special care and attention. Leadership interest, participation, support, commitment, and accountability were paramount in successfully implementing change and making it attainable, maintainable, and sustainable. The leaders in the organization did set the tone and led the path of change. They not only talked the talk, they also walked the walk, which was refreshing for me to witness.

I felt very proud to have made a difference for an industry, an organization, and a group of individuals about whom I was passionate. My area of study is at the forefront of national discussion, and I knew that I, as well as my study, was headed in the right direction. I could not have asked for anything more, and because I knew my topic of study so well, I was able to defend it with confidence and conviction. Chapter 5 brought everything together for me, and I was able to create scholarly research that was meaningful to me, the leaders, the participants, and my area of study.

Chapter 13: Defense: On Guard!

Leilani Longa

"The best defense is a good offense."

- Vince Lombardi

The dissertation defense is the process by which the committee examines the student's doctoral dissertation. During the examination, the committee evaluates the student's understanding, knowledge, intelligence, and competence as a scholarly researcher. The committee members inquire about areas of the dissertation study and provide consultation to the students. It is wise for students to prepare and anticipate questions in parts of the dissertation, whether through explaining the topic or content itself, the literature review, the study participants, or the findings of the dissertation. Careful planning, preparation, and practice will go far during the doctoral oral defense.

This chapter introduces the history and purpose of the doctoral defense as well as observations on the present day traditional and online defense. Additionally, this chapter offers guidance on preparing for a doctoral defense, beginning with selecting a defendable topic and extending to examining possible weak points and more. The chapter also provides information about the day of the defense and what to do after the completion of the oral defense: should the student choose to publish, present, or consider other opportunities? Students who wish to have a successful outcome to their doctoral dissertation defense will find this chapter as well as other chapters beneficial.

Purpose of the Doctoral Defense

It is important to understand the purpose of a doctoral defense as it involves evaluation of the student's competence in the dissertation study and research process. The student's written research and understanding of the topic are in an oral presentation to ensure the student has gained proficiency as an expert in the area of study and has developed the skills of a scholarly researcher. The oral defense allows the student to demonstrate a high level of knowledge and aptitude for scholarly research. During the doctoral oral defense, the committee and student review the dissertation and research study process, at times finding areas of improvement to build a stronger written dissertation.

Present Day Doctoral Defense

The present day doctoral defense for some students has changed from the traditional university setting to the online university setting. The traditional university oral defense is presented in person, whereas the online university oral defense is presented virtually. Students in both defense settings prepare presentations and use audiovisual materials to assist in their oral defense whether the aids include slides, a video presentation, or handouts. Both university settings include their own sets of benefits and challenges for doctoral students, but ultimately the processes are quite similar.

Traditional University Doctoral Defense

Traditional universities, where most oral defenses are conducted in person with the committee members and the student, are primarily formal. Student appearance, presentation skills, and verbal and non-verbal expressions are prominent during an in-person oral defense. There is no place to hide the student's physical and emotional behaviors. By the same token, the committee members are held to a similar level of exposure and awareness. Students should exude a level of confidence, professionalism, and expertise during this somewhat uncertain and uncomfortable time. Picture this moment as being like your first job interview: you are looking and feeling your best and preparing yourself in a manner that will allow you to land your dream job. It is all about you at this point, and nothing else matters—just the goal of getting the job—but in this case, passing your doctoral defense.

Online University Doctoral Defense

Online universities approach the defense process in a different way. Most often, the venue is via video conferencing, teleconferencing, or online conferencing. Online universities have set a precedent for applying technology and innovation into the world of academia. In contrast to a traditional in-person oral defense, the level of physical exposure is limited, depending on the selected method of hosting the virtual doctoral defense. Should the student use a communication method that does not allow the committee to see the student, the physical appearance factor disappears. However, the level of confidence, professionalism, and expertise can still resonate through the student's voice, as well as any background activity that may come through the speakers. In the cases of both the traditional and online doctoral oral defense, the student must be prepared.

Preparing Your Doctoral Defense

"Hence that general is skillful in attack whose opponent does not know what to defend; and he is skillful in defense whose opponent does not know what to attack."

- Sun Tzu

Preparing your doctoral defense is of the utmost importance. This is your last sprint to the finish line, and you can hear the roar of the crowd in the background. The cheer "You can do it!" should be a mantra in your head at this time. It is time for you to demonstrate your expertise and mastery in your field of study in research. Although this may seem like a simple task, students should take their time planning, preparing, and practicing for their big day in the spotlight.

Choosing a Defendable Topic

During year 2 residency, as shared in previous chapters, the student is expected to select a topic and have it approved. During this process, the instructor and student examine several research ideas and determine its value and relevance to scholarly research and its contribution to the literature. Students who are novices to research most often initially fall into two categories when gathering ideas for research topics. The first kind of student chooses a grandiose topic, something over the top. The second falls at the opposite end of the spectrum, selecting a topic that is minute or insignificant. Once the topic is accepted and approved, it sets the ball rolling to building a dissertation research study that is defendable.

Determining Who Will be Present

Similar to coordinating a meeting at work, it is important to determine that the appropriate people will be present at the oral defense. For the most part, your mentor and committee members are essential because they play a significant role in the oral defense. Although not formally invited, other individuals from the academic community may attend the oral defense as well. If you are unsure of whom to invite to the doctoral defense, consult your mentor.

Determining the Defense Format

Once the student has identified who will participate in the oral defense, it is time to plan the presentation format for the defense. The oral defense usually includes time for the student to present his research study and for the committee to comment and make inquiries about the research. A frequently asked question by students is what to include in the defense format. It is significant to include the main points of your dissertation and the highlights of your study. The extent of these points and the highlights include, but are not limited to, the problem and purpose statement, hypothesis, research questions, methodology, analysis, and findings. It is helpful to seek guidance from your mentor and advice from your cohort to determine what is expected in the defense format and the necessary requirements to include in your presentation.

Incorporating Your Defense into your Entire Research Process

The entire research process that each student experiences should be incorporated in the oral defense. Much of the defense is centered on the written dissertation and the actual research study process itself. It is important that you be aware of and capture the experiences you encounter as a researcher. Most of the student's research experience is explained in the methodology section of the dissertation. Reviewing and reliving the research experience overall incorporates the process into your defense.

Examining Potential Weak Areas Before the Defense

Students who are preparing for the defense should review their written dissertations and identify areas within their study that are vulnerable or potential weak points. One way to help determine the areas susceptible to scrutiny and questioning that are seen as *holes* in your research is to allow other cohort members, colleagues, or academic professionals to listen to and read your dissertation. Usually, this process will stimulate questions and requests for clarification about the research and will allow the student to become aware, to acknowledge, and to recognize the areas that may need a little more work. The student can then prepare for a line of questioning in these areas that the committee members may ask or call out. It is beneficial to the student to have the insight and ability to anticipate what will occur during the day of the oral defense.

Preparing for the Worst – Expecting the Best

It is a wise strategy for students to prepare for the worst and expect the best. This means to over-plan, over-prepare, and over-practice so that the student can cover as many vulnerable areas or points of contention as possible so that he or she is better prepared to answer completely unexpected questions or comments. The student's ability to be flexible with uncertainty and the unexpected during the defense is a talent within itself. Approaching the defense in a way that allows you to manage and handle questions and discussions as a learning process makes it easier to accept if you feel as though the defense went well or fell off track.

Set up a Defense Timeline/Things to do List

Students will find it beneficial to create a defense timeline when things happen throughout the dissertation process for a sense of how the dissertation flows into the defense process. Develop a "things to do list" to help in preparing for the big oral defense day. Establish a time frame for organizing your presentation, coordinating the logistics of the oral defense, making audiovisual materials, conducting mock presentations, reviewing the dissertation, and all other matters that will assist in planning for the day of defense. Keep this checklist with you so that you can check off items that have been completed as you approach the big day. If you do this, you will be organized and prepared so that if something comes along later that may have been missed, you will be able to pick up the pieces right away and not be side tracked with putting out fires or doing something else at the last minute.

Practice

Practice makes perfect, as the old saying goes, and practicing for your defense is no small feat. The ability to demonstrate knowledge of your study and to speak intellectually while demonstrating confidence and expertise on your topic is essential. Knowing the ins and outs of your study is one thing the committee looks for in the student. Students are encouraged to persuade their cohort members, colleagues, and mentors to spend time with them and rehearse the oral defense presentation before the day of the defense. As often as possible, practice and present the defense presentation with others until you feel comfortable and ready for defense day. During your rehearsals be cognizant of your tone, timing, and poise because whether the oral defense is in person or virtual, these actions are easily picked up by committee members and other observers. Recognizing these things during your practice presentations will help during the real oral defense.

The Defense Day

After all the practicing and perfecting of your oral presentation skills, the defense day is finally here. This is a good time to review and rehearse one last time, and then find your Zen. Center yourself so that you are balanced and able to manage your thoughts, emotions, nervousness, and any anxiety you may have. Take some time to meditate or distract yourself for the moment so as to take away the stress of the upcoming event. Leading up to the few minutes before the defense, dress to impress, and double check your appearance, gather your materials for the presentation, and put a smile on your face. You have been waiting for this day. You have dreamed about and visualized this day since you started your doctoral program. With confidence and courage, introduce yourself to the committee and others and begin your defense; nothing can stop you now.

Defense Over – Now What?

After a successful defense day, what is next? Many students present their doctoral dissertations to others at various events; some publish their dissertations, while others consult or teach what they have learned from their dissertations, and then others do nothing and treat their dissertations as a keepsake, representing a milestone they have accomplished in their life.

Whatever you choose to do next is completely up to you. However, it would be an unfortunate waste not to do anything with your newfound expertise as a scholarly researcher. Students are encouraged to present and/or publish their doctoral dissertation research.

Presenting

Presenting your dissertation findings is a good way to share your topic in order to gain visibility and exposure to professional and academic communities. Making presentations of all your hard work could boost your career aspirations and open new doors of opportunity you had not previously encountered or expected. When presenting your research, you are expected to reduce and trim down the content, as it would take a significant period of time to present the entire research study. Keep in mind the audience you are presenting to. Tailor the presentation to your audience, and whether you present to the Board of Directors of a company or to a roomful of professors at a university, know your audience.

Publishing

Publishing is a natural next step for doctoral researchers. Publishing your dissertation is one way of getting your name out there and allowing others to read your work and learn from your study. Other students may look to your dissertation study to begin their own work. If you are thinking about publishing, a number of journals may be appropriate to your research study. It is also helpful to question your committee, university faculty, or cohort members about publication in a journal. The following chapter provides more detailed information should you choose to publish after your defense.

Other

Some students choose to become experts in their area of study and may consult professionally, begin a new career, or teach in the world of academia. These opportunities present themselves often, during the doctoral process or after students have completed their dissertation and defense. From your doctoral experience, you will gain a level of knowledge and expertise that provides you with something that not all students obtain and that is a doctorate. This degree sheds light on a world and a future that you may not have previously known where new opportunities and choices come your way, and it sets you on a path to a new chapter in your life and career.

Personal Experiences

I did not know what to expect during my defense. The first thing I did was seek advice from my cohort. I was aware that some of my cohort members had already planned and presented their defenses. I believe that the best source of information is from those who have already experienced the journey. What I learned from each member with whom I spoke was that each had a different experience and a different expectation from his or her committee members. One member was drilled over and over about the validity and reliability of his study. Another person focused more on the content of the dissertation rather than on the results. And still another member of my cohort warned me to concentrate on the purpose and problem statement of the dissertation. Although this may sound discouraging, the point of unanimity among the three cohort members was the format of the defense. Incorporating the problem statement, purpose statement, research questions, and other sections previously discussed, I created a power point presentation with my dissertation highlights, allowing time for me to present and time for my committee to ask questions.

The one thing I had a bit of a panic about was how I was going to present my defense virtually. I did not know how to go about coordinating the event. Again, I sought advice from my cohort. I was then referred to a free online meeting site that allowed my committee members to call into a conference phone number and also have interactive access to present my oral defense presentation live, in real time. My committee members and I were able to have a discussion over the Internet. I learned something new using this new virtual free technology. This made life so much easier for me and eased my anxiety.

After preparing my presentation and coordinating the logistics of my defense, I sent my dissertation to my committee so that they could review, prepare, and participate in my defense. Not being able to see the faces and reactions of the committee was somewhat nerve-racking, but a relief at the same time. The virtual conference helped me to focus on my topic and on myself. I was asked about the process of my study, what I did and how I did it. During my defense the committee found areas in my dissertation that needed to be stronger, and through more discussion I was able to identify how I could include specific recommendations and suggestions into my dissertation. The one question I remember most was if I were to change anything during my study what would it be? I did identify one thing and that related to the allotted timeframe to conduct my study. In the length of time I had, I would have hoped to expand my study to include more participants. Overall, however, I did not experience any unexpected questions or comments.

During the defense, I felt very calm and confident, but once I had started, though I didn't realize it then, I began to speak a million miles an hour, and I was running through my slides quickly. My mentor actually had to interject and ask me to slow down and start over. I was a bit embarrassed, but at the same time I realized I was going through my slides very fast. I stepped back, took a deep breath, and started fresh. The remainder of my defense went so well and smoothly that by the end of the defense, I felt like I was among colleagues rather than before evaluators, trying to prove myself. I had shown my expertise and answered the questions with confidence. I had lived and breathed my dissertation study over a period of several months, and I knew if a question came my way that I had not expected, I would be able to answer it without hesitation.

As you go through the dissertation process and present your research study, students do, sometimes without realizing it, become experts in their topic, and that is something I experienced firsthand. My research became a part of me, and I knew it in my sleep. I believe that I had an advantage since I had selected a topic that was a current part of my career, and I knew that defending it would be something I could do with confidence. It became easy to talk about my study with intelligence and knowledge because I had grown into being a scholarly researcher. My level of maturity as a student and now as a research scholar became more obvious during the defense. I realized that I knew more than I had known, and it was such a revelation and validation to me. Some students may stumble through this process, but most intellectually work through the process, proving that they are now in a league amongst colleagues, scholars, experts, and educators. It is such a great feeling of accomplishment and satisfaction. My final thought after my doctoral oral defense was, *I have arrived!*

Chapter 14: What's Next? Getting Published!

Melanie Magruder with poem by Andy Elliott

How do I publish, you may eventually ask?

Getting published should be an easy task

Managing time and growing resources are necessary tricks –

To help the prolific author adjust very quick.

There is writing, editing, and more writing to be done.

The search for a publisher and deadlines remove some of the
fun.

From beginning to end, the process can be cumbersome

Leaving the excited author anxious and numb.

But.....if it is a goal of which you dream –

Stay fixed on the path and move with full steam.

We have all heard the saying – "If at first you don't
succeed......"

Try another route and follow all leads.

Your online doctoral program will publish your dissertation,

And then it will be available through libraries across the nation.

As far as articles, stories, or other ideas go –

There are a few suggestions you may wish to know.

Peer reviewed journals are an avenue some may take.

Yet they look for specific ideas – make no mistake –

If you are writing what they deem a good catch,

You may get lucky and find your article a perfect match.

If your article is forever world-changing in these modern times,

You may end up with a book deal rather than writing little
rhymes.

The trick to getting published is to do it on your own.

Online or in person find the company that throws the best
"bone."

What is the package price? Who will the illustrator be?

What are the fees that will suddenly affect me?

Some require money up front or give you a percentage of the
deal.

It all comes down to what you really want and how you feel.

Be sure to evaluate your resources and time –

Knowing that I published this with a specific reader in mind.

An Author and A Book Publisher

The Idea

As I sat looking out my window early one Saturday
morning or late Friday night after turning in another paper for

class, I pondered the thought, "What information or stories can I provide that will spark enough interest for a reader to purchase anything I may decide to write? How do I know if I have enough information for a book or an article?" These thoughts most likely cross the minds of many who may want to write and cannot decide whether to take that initial step. You will not know the answer to these questions until the idea you have is put on paper. I was told that everyone has a book to write and that I should never let doubt keep me from moving forward with the idea. I started writing, and within a year I was a published author.

While your dissertation is in the approval process with the dean's office, your mentor will probably suggest that you research a way to write and publish an article that is directly related to your research topic. There are many websites and periodicals that will publish articles based on your area of interest. At this point, you will have conducted a significant amount of research and have read many periodicals, peer reviewed material, and books. You are probably thinking, "What could I possibly write?" A lot of information can be extracted from your papers and dissertation. In this book, we told you not to try and "save the world; just get the paper completed." Now is when you can write what you really wanted to, but didn't because of time constraints, mentor pushback, etc. Write about what you want people to know. Somebody will read it.

Once you have decided on a topic for the book or article, research the idea. Find out what else has been written about the topic and focus on what has not. Seek an audience that is just waiting for your idea to be put on paper.

Do I Have the Experience?

Experience is gained by doing something. Once you start writing, you will be able to communicate your experience, and you will get published. You are already a writer because the dissertation is an original piece of work that can be published and copyrighted. If you are still not convinced, there are classes you can enroll in and mentors available to assist the new writer in becoming published. Just think about this for a moment. You just completed a major accomplishment, a dissertation. If that does not give you the experience, then what will? Many people do not attempt to write because they measure themselves against the great ones. You should start from where you are and—just write. Be yourself; you will be surprised because you could very well be a great writer.

Once you start writing, it would be a good idea to join a writing club or support group. There are many from which you can choose. The Internet is an important tool that will be a time saver in gaining the information needed to move forward. Take risks and remain committed to the goal.

How do I Sell my Idea?

When I had decided to write a book, the next thing that came to mind was publishing. How would I sell my idea? I was a doctoral candidate when I made the decision to write my first book. I pondered the idea because I did not know about publishing and thought that the only way to accomplish this goal was to sell my book through a publishing company. Little did I know about the world of self-publishing through On-Demand and small publishing houses.

As a doctoral student, the key component to my success was research. I was really good at it, and off I went to seek my options based on new discoveries and those that are familiar to most. After much review and consideration, I decided that self-publishing through On-Demand was the way to go for me. It was inexpensive, yet provided much exposure, which gave me the chance to get my feet wet and to determine if this was something I truly wanted to do without incurring a significant amount of time or costs.

On-Demand companies and small publishing houses are both excellent means for a first-time writer to get published without incurring a lot of costs or rejections from major publishing companies. Once you write it, if you know that it is a best seller, get an agent to help. If you are still not sure, sell it yourself, through online bookstores, your website, book clubs, and other mediums. Then after selling thousands of copies and acquiring positive reviews, seek an agent for consultation.

It would also be very beneficial to develop a promotional plan, beginning with a press release and posting it on free press release sites and other media available on the Internet. Building a website can be very inexpensive if you decide to do it yourself. Hiring someone to do it for you can cost a few hundred to several thousand dollars.

What Does Publishing Cost?

One of the main reasons I decided to self-publish through On-Demand was that the initial cost seemed reasonable. Although I had to pay for each copy of my book, a graphics designer and editor, there was no pre-set quantity that I needed to purchase, nor did I have to make a commitment to anyone other than myself. I hired a graphics designer and an editor to support the book idea, and the writing began. I would recommend hiring entrepreneurs to support your goals; their fees will be reasonable and affordable.

I did consider the small publishing house, but the upfront cost was nearly two times the cost of self-publishing through On-Demand. On-Demand has not been on the market very long, and it can be the solution for many self-published authors and small publishers. On-Demand printing allows the author to print only books that are ordered. Books are printed within two to three business days; shipping occurs shortly thereafter. You pay only for the books that are actually ordered. Though costs will vary by company, the average cost for printing 1 to 100 books through this method is approximately $3.50 per book and this is based on the retail price of your book. Using small publishing house printing methods, such an arrangement would normally require a commitment to print 1,000 to 2,500 books in order to get costs down to $3.50 per book.

On-Demand printing saves money in other ways, too. First, the author does not have to keep books in storage. Second, the On-Demand company is responsible for profits, so that the author does not have to run from bookstore to bookstore, performing the duties of a collection agent. Additionally, some On-Demand companies have distribution options, making your book available anywhere a book can be sold. Most On-Demand companies do charge a setup fee, which can run from $39 to approximately $300. After that, the only costs are for the actual printing. There may be additional costs for the distribution and marketing programs. However, any costs are relatively insignificant compared to the benefits offered by On-Demand publishing. On-Demand publishing helps the self-published author accomplish goals in a very inexpensive way.

You can take a chance and send the manuscript in to one of the bigger publishing companies and wait for validation from them. However, you will find that selling the book yourself will be faster and will gain more exposure for you, the writer. Big publishing companies have picked up some self-publishers after their books have gone on the shelves through On-Demand.

The pros and cons are basically up to the writer, because the options are plenty and you will have to weigh what works best. You do the research!

References

Allen, J. L., & Judd, B. B. (2007). Participation in decision-making and job satisfaction: Ideal and reality for male and female university faculty in the United States. *Human Communication, 10*(3), 157-179.

Andresen, M. A. (2009). Asynchronous discussion forums: Success factors, outcomes, assessments, and limitations. *Educational Technology & Society, 12*(1), 249-257.

Barker, David. (2010, August 27). *MSU to Offer Hybrid Online Doctorate Program*. Retrieved from http://www.statenews.com/index.php/article/010/02/msu_to_offer_hybrid_online_doctorate_program

Cashman, K. (2009). Authentic influence. *Leadership Excellence, 26*(10), p. 12. Retrieved from EBSCOhost.

Creswell, J. W. (2005). *Educational research: Planning, conducting, and evaluating quantitative and qualitative research* (2nd ed.). Thousand Oaks, CA: Sage Publications.

Creswell, J. (2007). Qualitative studies. San Francisco, CA: Sage Publications.

Common Editions of Sacred Texts. (2009-2010). *The University of Washington Libraries.* Retrieved from http://guides.lib.washington.edu/content.php?pid=56714&sid=989070

Conrad, K. A. (2007). Description of UOP academic review board. Academic Review Board Reviewer Training ePack.

Ely, S. (2007, Winter). Reading Level. *Lambda Book Report, 14*(4), pp. 22-24.

Fox, J. C. (1999). What is an Executive Order? *American Government & Politics Online.*

www.ehow.com/how_5909425_pay-phd-education.html

Golde, C. M., & Dore, T. M. (2001). *At cross purposes: What the experiences of doctoral students reveal about doctoral education.* Philadelphia, PA: Pew Charitable Trusts. Retrieved from www.phd-survey.org

Horsburgh, D. (2003). Evaluation of qualitative research. *Journal of Clinical Nursing, 12*(2), 307-312. Retrieved from EBSCOhost.

Levi, D. (2007). *Group dynamics for teams.* (2nd ed.). Thousand Oaks, CA: Sage Publications.

Littlefield, J. (n.d.). *Online college residency requirements.* Retrieved October 11, 2010, from http://distancelearn.about.com/od/distancelearning101/p/ResidencyReq.htm

Mayadas, F. (1997, March). Asynchronous learning networks: A Sloan Foundation perspective. *Journal of Asynchronous Learning Networks, 1*(1), 1-16.

McMillan, J. H., & Schumacher, S. (2006). *Research in education: Evidence-based inquiry* (6th ed.). New York, NY: Pearson.

Merriam-Webster online. (n.d.) Retrieved March 22, 2010, from

http://www.merriam-webster.com/dictionary/time

Milligan, R., & Murray, V. C. (2000, July/August). Black issues book review. *2*(4), 65-67.

Morse, K. (2003, February). Does one size fit all? Exploring asynchronous learning in a multicultural environment. *Journal of Asynchronous Learning Networks, 7*(1), 37-55.

Neuman, W. L. (2003). *Social research methods: Qualitative and quantitative approaches* (5th ed.). Boston, MA: University of Wisconsin.

New Mexico State University (2010). *How to pay for a PhD.* Retrieved from

http://education.nmsu.edu/emd/docpage.html

Owens, R. R. (2002). *E-Learning at Boston College: Classic Education Meets 21st Century Technology.* Retrieved from http://www.elearn mag.org/subpage.cfm? section=case_studies&article=32-1

Smarty, A. (2010, July). *History of Online Education*. Retrieved from http://www.historyofonlineeducation.com.

The Early History of Christianity. (n.d). *The Historian*. Retrieved from http://www.historian.net/jesused.html

Tuckman, B., & Jensen, M. (1977). Stages of small group development revisited. *Group and Organizational Studies, 2*, 419-427.

Vaill, P. (1996). *Learning as a way of being: Strategies for survival in a world of permanent white water*. San Francisco, CA: Jossey-Bass.

Washburn, N. T., DeLuque, M. S., & Waldman, D. A. (2007). Follower perceptions of CEO leadership as a function of the leader's stakeholder and economic values. *Academy of Management Proceedings 1-6*.

Yin, R. K. (2003). Case study and research: Design and methods (3rd ed.).Thousand Oaks, CA: Sage.

About the Authors

Dr. Sybil DeVeaux is a professor of management at the Empire State College where she also mentors undergraduate students. Additionally, she mentors a doctoral student at the University of Phoenix, Arizona. A lifelong educator, Dr. DeVeaux has also taught at the elementary and junior high school levels. She holds papers from Cambridge University (GCE) with a distinction in English Literature; a teacher's certificate from Mico Teacher's College, Jamaica; a BA from Baruch College, New York; a Master's degree (MA) from Brooklyn College, New York; and a doctorate in Leadership Management from the University of Phoenix, Arizona. Dr. DeVeaux's dissertation focused on barriers that Eastern Caribbean immigrants experience in advancement to civil service leadership positions. Dr. DeVeaux resides with her family in Brooklyn, New York.

Dr. Andy Elliott is an upper elementary teacher at Pedley Elementary School in the Jurupa Unified School District. He has worked in Riverside, California, with culturally and linguistically diverse students for almost 20 years. He is a mentor teacher, administrative designee (assistant principal), and Title I Coordinator. He currently teaches sixth grade. In his spare time, he facilitates undergraduate and graduate classes for the University of Phoenix and The City University of Seattle. He was named Teacher of the Year in 2006 (a big honor as he was nominated and elected by his peers and principal). He has a Master's Degree in Special Education and an Administrative Services Credential. As of June 2008, he accomplished his final education goal and completed his doctorate in Educational Leadership. That is what has led his to this adventure—collaborating and writing a practical guide for the on-line doctoral student, *Full Speed Ahead*. He has also published an educational guide for dealing with student interventions, *Inclusion Implemented Effectively*, and an inspirational book, *Instead of Chocolate*. His areas of expertise include interventions, special education, classroom management, and working with EL (English learners) students.

Dr. Leilani Longa is a healthcare professional with over 12 years of experience in hospital and clinic operations. With expertise in leadership and organizational development, knowledge management, process improvement, and strategic planning, Dr. Longa has played a key role in implementing best practices, improving operational services, and deploying a state of the art electronic medical record and physician support system. Currently, Dr. Longa is project managing the operational building and designing of a new Healthcare Medical Center in the Northwest with Kaiser Permanente. As a healthcare leader, she is dedicated to providing the highest quality of care using innovative technology and excellence in service. Dr. Longa holds a Master's Degree in Management from Hawaii Pacific University and a Doctor of Management in Organizational Leadership from the University of Phoenix.

Dr. Melanie Magruder has more than 16 years of leadership experience in corporate business, customer relations, mentoring and coaching, corporate training, community and social outreach, and a record of successful job performance. An accomplished business strategist and marketer, her vision and expertise in business performance have driven notable growth in the technology and social services industries. Offering a rare blend of creative and operational strengths, Dr. Magruder has achieved exciting progress in developing and implementing community projects and is recognized for her success in growing business relationships and partnerships. Her strategic approach to building a business is reflected in her work as Executive Director/President of All Empowered, Inc., a nonprofit, community-based organization where her concept creation and focus on community and social development deliver impressive results. Dr. Magruder also owns and operates an Image and Leadership Consulting Service, Empower Us, Inc., where her clientele consists of businesses in the United States and Europe. Dr. Magruder's exceptional track record of business improvement is based on her philosophy of total community engagement in change. She is known for her ability to quickly identify and diagnose growth impediments in the community and business relations. Dr. Magruder received her BS degree in Computer Information Systems from Saint Leo University, an MBA in Healthcare Management, and a Doctorate in Management of Organizational Leadership from the University of Phoenix. Dr. Magruder is a published author, book publisher, active public speaker, and workshop facilitator. She is a member of Project Management Institute (PMI), Toastmasters International (TI), Women In Technology (TI), and the American Society for Quality (ASQ). She resides in the Atlanta Metropolitan area.

Dr. Cheryl Szyarto is certified as a public school principal as well as a teacher of the Handicapped (grades K-12) and an elementary teacher (grades K-8) in New Jersey. In addition to her associate faculty positions with two regionally accredited universities, The University of Phoenix and The City University of Seattle, she serves as a Faculty Site Supervisor for University of Phoenix student teachers in New Jersey and Pennsylvania. Having earned honors on both state and national levels for special education teaching excellence, Dr. Szyarto is a lifelong learner and researcher committed to developing and delivering high quality, technology-driven instructional programs that cater to the unique needs of adult students. She holds a B.A. in psychology and an M.A. Ed. in Elementary/Special Education from Rutgers University (NJ); she has served as a Princeton University (NJ) teacher scholar, and earned her Ed.D. in Educational Leadership from The University of Phoenix (AZ). Her dissertation involved an ethnographic collective case study, which focused on the collaborative leadership experiences of general education teachers working alongside paraprofessional staff in K-5 inclusion classrooms. She is also a contributing author to a City University of Seattle publication project titled, *Proven Practices in Higher Education: Strategies to Improve Online Learning and Assessment for Adult Students*; the text is scheduled for release in the spring of 2011. While Dr. Szyarto has invested her years as an educator/educational leader in the New Jersey school systems (public and private sectors) for the past ten years, she currently resides in Central Bucks County, Pennsylvania, with her husband and three children.

Dr. Ed S. Turner III is the author of *Increasing Employee Involvement*. A former football player in college, where he first learned the importance of teamwork, Dr. Turner is a retired Army Colonel with a bachelor's degree in Business Administration from Trinity University, a master's degree in Organizational Communication from the University of Northern Colorado, a Master of Military Science from the Command and General Staff College, Fort Leavenworth, Kansas, a doctorate in Military Science, Air War College, Maxwell Air Force Base, and a doctorate of Management in Organizational Leadership from The University of Phoenix. He has held positions of increasing authority in the military where he brought a broad operational and strategic vision to large-scale troop maneuvers. Dr. Turner holds numerous meritorious service medals; he served mostly during the Cold War. In the civilian sector Dr. Turner has 25 years of experience as a management development trainer and shaper of organizational change. Dr. Turner holds certifications in Human Resource Law, Developmental Dimensions International Leadership Facilitator, Small Group Facilitator/Trainer, Benchmark Facilitator, Organizational Development Facilitator, Quality Circle Facilitator, Change Management Facilitator, Experiential Workshop Developer, and Leadership, Management and Development Trainer. Dr. Turner resides with his wife, Victoria, in Centennial, Colorado. They have four adult sons and six grandchildren. Dr. Turner works for the Federal Government in veteran healthcare and spends most of his off time as a member of Cherry Hills Community Church supporting Christian ministries and efforts to end homelessness in the Denver Metro Area.